RELENTLESS, ENVIOUS DEATH:

The Biographies of
Katherine Shaw Bethea
Solomon Hicks Bethea

A.K. Thompson

First printing 2013

Printed in the United States of America
ISBN 978-0-9851640-0-3

"Biographies are but the clothes and buttons of the man. The biography of the man himself cannot be written."

~ Mark Twain

This book is dedicated to all of the nurses, doctors and staff of Katherine Shaw Bethea Hospital ~ past, present, and future.

Foreword

As the President and CEO of Katherine Shaw Bethea Hospital, I had the privilege of working with a wonderful staff to make KSB one of the best small hospitals in the Nation. However, KSB did not just 'appear' out of the ether—it was KSB's rich history—what little I knew of it anyway, that made me want to learn the story of the people *behind* KSB. Our marketing department coined a slogan for the hospital "KSB—It's the People" and for many of us who worked there it was our "Aunt Katherine" who steered so many of our decisions and who was our moral compass if you will.

I've always been a genealogy enthusiast so I began asking myself a few questions: *Who was Katherine Shaw Bethea? And what of her husband, Solomon Hicks Bethea, who established the hospital in her name?* Every good story begins by asking some good questions and we didn't have many answers to those about Katherine and Solomon.

In October of 2005 I first approached the author about a book project. Since I knew her father, I had learned that she not only had recently returned from California with a Master's Degree in Creative Writing, but that she also held a Bachelor's Degree in Journalism. I knew that it would take someone like her with not only writing skills—but with extensive researching skills to undertake this project. I knew all-too-well how difficult it can be to track down the past and make sense of it all from doing my own family's genealogical research.

When we started the project we thought we could knock it out in maybe a year or so. Quickly, both the author and I learned that it was to be no simple task. As chapters slowly came across my desk I was stunned at just how important KSB Hospital really is—I couldn't believe how these people, our founders and benefactors, began to come to life again after over a hundred years. We began to find out just how truly remarkable these two people were.

This book is not merely a double biography of Katherine and Solomon; it also paints the wonderful history of life in early Dixon. From Dixon's roots in farming, to her ties with the famous plow-king of Moline, John Deere—from a terrible murder that occurred south of town, which spurred the most infamous street name in Dixon—*Bloody Gulch Road*—to our town's and the Bethea's ties with Presidents and Statesmen, this book is far more than a simple biography.

At the end of the day, I believe this book is very much a love story. KSB Hospital is a wonderful gift from a husband to the young wife he could not save. Solomon Hicks Bethea, while having an impressive legal and political career, never lost sight of his hometown and the people he loved. Katherine Shaw Bethea Hospital is here because Solomon did not want others in Dixon to suffer the lack of care his wife endured during her years-long struggle with tuberculosis.

Solomon knew that Katherine's life was prolonged due to the quality of care she received in places like Denver, Colorado and Asheville, North Carolina. He also knew that the only reason she received such care is because they could afford it—something he also knew most people of Dixon could not.

Solomon made sure there would be a place in Dixon where everyone—from the financially sound to the poor—could receive top-of-the line medical care.

Katherine Shaw Bethea Hospital still proudly carries out the mission Solomon set forth in the late 1800's—to give this community the best healthcare experience possible, and to ensure a healthy and happy Dixon, Illinois. I was privileged to play a leadership role at the hospital for over 28 years after our family moved to Dixon from Wisconsin in 1983. The Vandervorts are proud to serve Dixon and call it home, and I'm sure that Solomon and Katherine would be proud of this book. I want to thank A.K. Thompson for what a great job she did in capturing the spirit of KSB Hospital through this history of its two main benefactors. I sincerely hope you enjoy as much as I did finding out about the Bethea's.

Darryl Vandervort
CFO of KSB from 1983 - 1988
President and CEO of KSB from 1989 - 2011

Contents

Editor's Notes

Relationships are the drivers of many things. They can be cause of both good and bad. In the case of Solomon Hicks Bethea and Katherine Shaw Bethea their relationship was one of a complex of issues of disease, career, politics, community and most importantly, love. Throughout their too brief time together and Solomon's ensuing years alone following Katherine's early demise from tuberculosis they remained focused on a sense of shared humanity and a desire to lovingly support each other and help the broader community who they both saw as less fortunate than themselves.

It is because this book examines these two lives and the families from which they came that we can begin to understand just how deeply they cared. We can understand that this caring went well beyond each other and how ultimately it manifested itself in their lasting gift of Katherine Shaw Bethea Hospital or as it is known today, KSB.

This is a tale of two individuals, two extended families and is woven around the interesting history of their time. Now that over one hundred years have lapsed since Solomon Bethea's death and the hospital's name is shortened to KSB it is important to reflect upon who these people were, where they came from, what they stood for, what they accomplished, what mattered most to each of them, what others and the community meant to both and what they meant for and to each other. Here lies the true story of Kittie and Solie Bethea.

XVII

Acknowledgements

Writing a book is no easy task, and what you are holding in your hands is no exception. What began as an assumed "simple" book quickly turned into a monumental undertaking. The research for this double-biography took nearly three years to complete and involved an over 3,000 mile tour of the South visiting source locations, hours of pouring over historical texts and the help of a large number of truly remarkable people. This book is the vision of former KSB Hospital President, Darryl Vandervort. Mr. Vandervort has consistently been a champion for Dixon, Illinois, and Katherine Shaw Bethea Hospital. Stemming from his love of genealogy, Mr. Vandervort realized the importance of the story of the people *behind* KSB Hospital. To have such a quality hospital in Dixon is quite a gift, so Mr. Vandervort approached the author in 2005 with a single purpose in mind: To tell the story of the people who gave that fine gift to the community.

First and foremost, the author would like to thank the Lee County Historical and Genealogical Societies and volunteers for their assistance during the extensive project research. It must also be noted here, with great gratitude, that without the archive of the *Dixon Evening Telegraph* and the *Telegraph* newspaper, it would have simply been impossible to write this book. The *Dixon Evening Telegraph* was founded in 1851 and in 1995 the publisher purchased the *Daily Gazette* in Sterling, Illinois and formed Sauk Valley Newspapers to operate both papers and others owned across northern Illinois. The name of the Dixon paper was shortened to the *Telegraph* at that time and for consistency in this book all references will be to the *Telegraph*. An unbelievable amount of information contained within these pages is sourced directly from the *Telegraph*, and the author is eternally grateful for the use of this information that made the story of Solomon and Katherine Bethea truly come to life. The *Amboy Journal* also was a significant source for information contained within these pages, and the author is thankful for those archived materials as well.

The list of individuals and associations that aided in the creation of this narrative is extensive. The author, in no particular order will list those persons who directly helped, whether by looking into archives and making copies to send, or simply offering a great conversation about the past. The author greatly regrets if she has left anyone off of the list.

Kristen Dubay for help with the North Carolina Medical Journal citation information; Carlton Smith for all his wonderful help with the Bethea reunion in Woodberry, Arkansas, and of course the entire Bethea Clan, namely Gene and Fran Bethea, Bill Blann and Sammie Minchew, who made the author feel right at home when she showed up on the doorstep of the reunion hall unannounced; Malgosia Myc and the entire research department at The Bentley Historic Library at The University of Michigan; The Marion County Historic Library and Archives of South Carolina; Jeffrey A. Lovett for wonderful photographs; Pat Gorman and Bob Gibler for all their assistance in Lee County history; Wallace Dailey of the Houghton Library at Harvard College who helped locate information from the Theodore Roosevelt Collection; Anne M. Huber, librarian at the Illinois State Geological Survey; Christopher Payne for his help with Silsbee research; Bernadine Deckard and

Bruce Whitmore for the lovely letter written to Solomon from his aunt (and our wonderful phone conversations, Bernadine); Roger D.K. Thomas and John Williamson Nevin of The Paleontological Society with The Department of Earth and Environment at Franklin & Marshall College in Lancaster, Pennsylvania; Sherrie Kline Smith with the Missouri Valley Special Collections; Elizabeth Forbes of Illinois College; The Missouri State Archives; Christina Sebastian, Director of Alumni Affairs for Albany Law School; The Loveland Museum of Dixon, Illinois; Gordon Johnson for spending an afternoon scanning photos for the book; Fran Swarbrick for her immensely helpful hands; The Dixon Public Library; Jean Yong of The Monadnock Building, Chicago; Susan R. Lewis at the Charles Deering McCormick Library at Northwestern University and Sigrid Pohl Perry, Ph.D.; Bob Cavanagh, Cheryl Schnirring and Jan Perone of The Abraham Lincoln Presidential Library; Tony Ziselberger of The National Academy of Sciences; Kermit Moore for his fine reading of drafts of the book and literary conversations; Mike Symanski for his unrelenting belief in and appreciation of the arts and the countless hours of conversation about how important it is to write and create; Jenny LeMoine for her wonderful friendship and support; Jesse Dale Caraway; and a big, big thank you to Michele Carr, Tom Demmer and Marjorie Lundquist of Katherine Shaw Bethea Hospital.

Importantly, the author would like to thank her wonderful family – John, Debbie and Christopher Thompson for all their support, enthusiasm and encouragement of this project. If it weren't for their continued interest in the research and writing of this book, you would not be holding it in your hands.

XXII

Chapter 1

From Ireland, *or Scotland*, to Lee County:
The Shaw Family

Katherine Shaw Bethea, the daughter of Samuel and Mary Campbell Shaw, was born in 1855 in Palmyra, Illinois. The youngest of eight children, she no doubt had a very busy childhood growing up on the farm.

Katherine was a horse enthusiast, very well versed in the equestrian sport. In one mention in the local newspaper, she and Solomon rode to Sterling on horseback, leaving early in the morning and dined at the Galt House. At the conclusion of this note, the *Daily Gazette* wrote, "Mrs. Bethea's horse is a superior riding animal and she rides with a gracefulness seldom equaled by ladies."

She was also very involved in nearby Dixon community affairs, serving as a committee woman for The Farmer's Institute, as a member of the Phidian Art Club and the Columbian Club, as well as a supporter of The Opera House, sharing her passion for theater and often delivering speeches in favor of the importance of the arts in Dixon.

Katherine was also a consummate hostess. During the summer of 1885, she and Solomon lived in the Nachusa House, which was noted as being truly accommodating and modern and where "choice Sunday dinners" were served. The *Telegraph* wrote of these events that, "our citizens have taken quite kindly to these dinners."

The Nachusa House was the social hub of Dixon during this time, hosting many events and catering to top political officials during their travels through the area, and had guests who included the likes of Abraham Lincoln.

In celebration of the fall season in Dixon, Solomon and Katherine hosted a party on a Tuesday evening in September, for which her oldest brother James traveled from Mount Carroll. Almost 150 people attended the event and the following day it was said of the party that, "none to follow will probably be more thoroughly enjoyed."

Another period mention of Katherine came during one of her countless trips for her health to Colorado with Solomon when she was injured while exiting a buggy. The horses reared back, causing the wheel of the carriage to roll over her foot and breaking her ankle. She made a speedy recovery after spending a week on bed rest. This was just one incident mentioning her time spent away from Dixon. The couple traveled often for the sake of her poor health associated with tuberculosis. They frequented Colorado, but also spent a summer in Las Vegas, New Mexico, and eventually she sought respite in Asheville, North Carolina. Katherine also accompanied Solomon to Chicago on a few occasions when he had to travel for business.

Her siblings, in order of oldest to youngest, were as follows: James; William; Archibald; Timothy; Samuel Jr.; Elizabeth, and Mary Anna.

According to many historical records, the Shaw family emigrated from Ireland to the United States in the early 1830's. There are many discrepancies however, contained in census records, obituaries and biographical sketches, stating that they came from Scotland. Both surnames, Campbell and Shaw take their root from Scottish clan names but there is no way to be sure they came from Scotland, as so many families traveled between European countries and immigration records have not been located. The home country of Ireland is recorded many times, as is Scotland, and perhaps the Shaw's originated in Scotland, traveled to Ireland, where Katherine's mother Mary gave birth to James, and from there crossed the Atlantic Ocean to the United States.

As pure speculation, one could come to the conclusion that at times the census man came to the home, when parents were not present and one of the children answered the questions to the best of their ability. It is easy to understand how this could happen, as Samuel Sr. was frequently in the fields working his cattle, probably with the older boys and Mary could have been away in town shopping or running other errands. This would have left the younger children at home.

For instance, in the census year of 1850, Archibald was the youngest boy at age 11, and not yet working the fields with his father and brothers James and William, so perhaps he was the only one home to answer the family questions, mistaking the country of origin. This is merely a theory however, as the census did not reflect them coming from Scotland until 1880, and the reason for this abrupt change is very curious, as all subsequent census reports indicate Scotland as their homeland.

Another theory as to the early discrepancies rests again on the shoulders of the census taker. It is not far-fetched that the census man could not discern between an Irish or Scottish accent, and recorded the country of origin based on his own assumptions alone. Simply, early census records were not a model of precision or accuracy.

Regardless of where the Shaw family came from, they arrived in Cass County, Illinois around 1833 as pioneers. From there they moved north to Lee County around 1855. Samuel Sr. was a farmer and raised stock on what would later become the Village of Prairieville, which was built on one corner of the family farm.

Katherine's father: Samuel Shaw Sr.

Katherine's father, Samuel Shaw Sr. was born sometime around 1803. Barring the information gleaned from census records; there are few mentions of Samuel and Mary Shaw. There are accounts of two land purchases in Cass County, Illinois on November 1, 1839. The deeds from the General Land Office of Springfield, under the administration of President Martin Van Buren, list Mr. Shaw as coming from Morgan County. Morgan is located on the southern border of Cass county and this demonstrates the possibility of the Shaw residence being somewhere along the southern border of Cass County.

He purchased some 80 acres total in two 40-acre tracts. In the mid-1800s the average cost of one acre of land was around $1.25. Samuel paid for the land in cash: $100. Since Samuel was very active in the farming and livestock trade, he surely owned more than 80 acres, and he would have sold this land when he relocated his large family to Lee County, where he purchased a large amount of land in Palmyra, Illinois.

An interesting illustration of early Palmyra life as mentioned in *Recollections of the Pioneers of Lee County* was published by the Columbian Club under the watchful, enthusiastic eye of Elizabeth Shaw and paints a picture of a typical Sunday church service.

The 1,000 inhabitants of Palmyra were spread far and wide across the county. The Sunday church service was rarely called to order on time as many large families traveled some distance to attend church. Many arrived by horse and buggy and a few by ox-drawn wagons. The recollection makes mention of these large oxen tethered by heavy chain to the trees surrounding the churchyard. It is interesting and a bit comical to imagine this scenario today, and one can picture Samuel and family speaking with friends after church, while these lumbering beasts of burden munched grass in the Sunday shade.

One interesting write-up about Samuel appeared in the *Dixon Sun* on Wednesday, April 24, 1872. The story begins, "Mr. Samuel Shaw of Palmyra met with quite an accident Tuesday morning last, while driving to town." Driving, of course, referred to driving his team of horses. The whiffletree, which is the revolving horizontal crossbar that attaches to the harness traces of a draft animal and then to the vehicle itself, broke, causing the horses to become unmanageable and start to run.

Samuel, unable to manage the horses, clung for dear life to the lines until his team ran up an embankment and overturned the buggy. Samuel dislocated his shoulder in the accident, and being a mile from any house, he waited there in a fair amount of pain, until a man happened by and drove him to town where Dr. Steele administered chloroform and, "the bone was soon put in position." All this, and Samuel was 69 years old. No doubt his years of hard work in the business of farming had made him a tough, weathered man, who probably didn't bat an eye during the whole ordeal.

An interesting side note regarding Samuel is included in a biographical sketch of Leon Shaw, Samuel's grandson by Archibald, in a history of Montana, and states that Samuel was a "personal friend of Abraham Lincoln." However, this is the only mention of such a relationship existing. It has been reported though that Lincoln was in the area around the end of July in 1860, at which time he took what would later be called a 'historic ride' on what would become the famous Lincoln Highway with Dixon resident, Joseph Crawford. It is entirely possible that Samuel could have at least met Abraham Lincoln then.

Samuel was instrumental in the formation of Prairieville, which was located and platted by Samuel, Abijah Powers, Phillip Schock and Winthrop Seavey on April 10, 1855. The all-important blacksmith shop was located there, and according to *The History of Lee County*, was running at top speed to service the horse and machinery needs of local farmers.

The first Civil War soldier's monument in Lee County, which cost about $900 to construct, was erected in Prairieville on June 3, 1869. This was the first monument in Lee County to commemorate the soldiers who lost their lives in the "War of the Rebellion." The monument was relocated in September of 1902 to, of all places, the Shaw family plot in the cemetery one half-mile north of Prairieville. There it remains today, commanding a view of the ornate wrought iron cemetery entrance.

Prairieville Cemetery
Lee County Civil War Memorial
Photo by J. Thompson

Katherine's brother Timothy was the first from Lee County to enlist in the Civil War, first killed and was buried at Prairieville, but his remains were later moved to the Shaw/Bethea plot in Oakwood Cemetery. Solomon Bethea delivered the keynote address at the rededication of the monument, which bore the names of all Palmyra soldiers who served in the war. Timothy's name is not listed on the Civil War Veterans Memorial bronze in the Lee County Court House because he was attending school in southern Illinois at the time of his enlistment at Jacksonville. He was never acknowledged as coming from Lee County. This is something of a cruel irony that the first Lee County son lost in the Civil War is not recognized among the others on the county's memorial listing.

Detail from Lee County Civil War Memorial Prairieville
Engraved with the names of the Shaw brothers
Timothy, Samuel and Archibald
Photo by J. Thompson

Katherine's mother: Mary Campbell

Katherine's mother, Mary Campbell Shaw was born around 1810. She passed away on Sunday, May 16, 1897, six years after Samuel died at 88 in August of 1891. The couple had left the farm and moved to Dixon in the early 1880's, where they had a home on the corner of Ottawa and 4th streets. The only written account of Mary was her obituary, which appeared in the *Telegraph*. She passed away in the Ottawa Avenue home, after a long illness at the age of 87. She, like many other farm women of the era, and as noted in all census records, spent her life "keeping house." This, however, certainly did not define her character. She was remembered as a very intelligent woman who, "nevertheless chose the domestic circle as her sphere in life."

She was dedicated to her large family in every respect, and must have been an incredibly strong woman to have weathered a journey across the Atlantic and spent all of her days as a devoted wife and mother to a pioneer family traveling the expanse of the early Illinois countryside. The Shaw's lost not one young or infant child to illness, as so many couples did in these times, perhaps as a result of her heartiness as a woman and her doting, watchful nature over all her eight children.

The Shaw's eldest son, James was born in Ireland on May 3, 1832 according to his obituary and death certificate. He went on to graduate from Illinois College at Jacksonville, where he studied law. He then located to Mt. Carroll, Illinois, and practiced law for many years. He also held office as Assistant State Geologist for three years and surveyed many counties in northern Illinois.

His published survey of Lee County not only reflects his unquenchable thirst for knowledge and understanding of the Illinois terrain, it also expresses his unique gift of eloquence with the written word.

In 1868 James made a geological survey of northwestern Illinois including Jo Daviess, Stephenson, Carroll, Winnebago, Boone, Ogle, Lee, Whiteside, Bureau, Henry, Marshall and Putnam Counties. The surveys, comprising over 200 pages, were published in 1873, and although his descriptions of all the counties are enjoyable and visceral in their presentation, here special consideration is given to his account of Lee County. In reading his words, one can easily imagine Katherine and Solomon riding their horses over the rolling plains, taking in all the beauty of Lee County.

James not only made it a point to transcribe the geological characteristics of Lee County, he expressly made notation of items of particular historic interest and offered invaluable visual descriptions of the landscape and wildlife.

In his opening descriptions of Lee County, James made special mention of the Osage Orange, a variety of hedge that was used in place of fencing on many farms throughout the area. The hedge is very prickly and thick, and when properly maintained and planted, "...would defy a buffalo to break through them." However, for a period of time the hedge was poorly cultivated and its use thus began to fade into obscurity, the few remaining rows unevenly grown and ragged, deforming the landscape. James made note of his pleasure in seeing the hedge's slow return as a fencing material, as its "long lines of well-grown, compact, green shining walls," graced the landscape of Lee County. James, well-aware that this tidbit of information was of little consequence to the geology of Illinois, wrote, "Hedge-growing and timber-growing are not geological questions, but they are great material interests."

Another instance of James' insistence to go beyond his call of duty as Assistant State Geologist is eloquently demonstrated in his description of the Winnebago swamps.

"No habitations are near these watery jungles. A spirit of desolation seems to brood over them. The tall, purple-caned reeds bend their light feathery tops in the wind; triangular-shaped rushes cut the bare legs of the wader with their sickle edges...and when the adventurous duck-hunter discharges his gun, the roar of myriads of wings, and an uprising cloud of the whole web-footed tribe, disclose the fact that even these desolate spots have their uses."

Another point of great local, as well as historic paleontological interest, lies in the fact that fellow 19th Century geologists Meek and Worthen discovered and named a new fossil species with Dixon, Illinois in mind. *Vanuxemia dixonensis* is a long extinct fossil bivalve (clam) that made its home in the murky deep

11

of Trenton Sea. Today, that Ordovician sea bottom and its inhabitants are recorded in outcrops of the 465 million year old Trenton Limestone, along the beautiful bluffs of the Rock River.

Surely many a scholar would be hard-pressed to locate another geological survey in which the geologist quotes Shakespeare, and perhaps James Shaw, in his unyielding talent for written expression, is the only one to take such pains in writing a survey; although it can be assumed that such utterances came easily for him. In his writing of the fossil remains in the Galena, Trenton and Buff limestone's of the area, his passion for history and propensity to make particular efforts in reader engagement are keenly demonstrated.

"We tread reverently among these old stones, marked with forms of life now fossilized; for a great chapter of the history of the earth—of the story of creation—lies half revealed before us. The entombment of relics of millions of years—cycles in which man had no part—Sibyline [*sic*] mysteries, almost too great for the finite mind to grasp—the story of indefinable epochs, written by the finite finger of the Creator, in strong traces – these and kindred thoughts come over us, when gathering the fossils. No wonder Shakespeare could find 'sermons in stones.' The stones are full of sermons; full of an inspired revelation; they are the great Bible of Creation—the Stone Book, whose solid leaves are pictured over with sublime truths."

James also authored the article, "Monograph of Antiquities," (Smithsonian Institute, Washington) which explored the mound builders of the Rock River valley and northern Illinois. The article is a fascinating look at the region's earliest occupants.

James demonstrated incredible ability as an orator as well as a writer. His profound talent with the pen can be seen in many of his publications, and especially in one speech he delivered in front of the Illinois House of Representatives during the military occupation aftermath of the Great Chicago fires of Tuesday evening January 24, 1872. The speech itself, 18 pages in length, is no doubt among the most insightful and reflective speeches ever delivered in front of the Illinois House.

A marked example of James' command of the English language is strongly demonstrated in reading the compelling words of the final paragraph. His poetic and visually illustrative closing remarks on the military occupation of Chicago no doubt offered cause for reflection in the House, and reason for great consideration among its members.

"When the new Chicago shall rise Phoenix like from her ashes, and the recollection of her calamitous days shall pass into history – when in some future time the story of the great blow to her active energies and great business capacities shall wander down along the ages, may the people of some straggling State or municipality, whose liberties are threatened by some irregular exercise of power, be able to point to the precedent we are now making, when, with charity to all, we utter our firm, kind and manly protest against the encroachments of the military upon the civil power – when, as in duty bound, we sustain the protest of our Governor in the conscious discharge of a painful duty, and feel unwilling that he should be sacrificed upon the smoking ruins of the great conflagration."

In 1872 James was chosen as a Presidential Elector on the Republican ticket. He served four terms as a Representative in the General Assembly and was elected Speaker of the House for the 1876 session. In 1891 he was elected Judge of the Circuit Court, and was re-elected in 1897, serving until his retirement in June of 1903. From *"1904 History of Lee County, Illinois," Mr. A.C. Bardwell.*

James A. Shaw, '57
Courtesy of Illinois College at Jacksonville Collection

14

Judge James A. Shaw presides in Lee County court
Courtesy of Loveland Collection

In June of 1859 James married Jennie Harvey of Wheeling, West Virginia. Jennie kept a fine garden, which was regarded by the people of Mount Carroll as the most beautiful, and the "talk of the town." She would, without any hesitation, give flowers to any townsfolk who wanted a centerpiece for their kitchen table or for transplant into their own yards. Together they had three children, Undine, Hoyt and Effie.

Effie, much like her father, was an incredibly smart young woman. She attended Vassar College and was valedictorian of her class. After graduation she was awarded a scholarship to an academy in Rome, but for unknown reasons did not attend, and stayed in Mount Carroll where she lived with her sister until her death in 1946.

James' daughter Undine passed away several years previous to her sister Effie and brother Hoyt Shaw moved to Southern Pines, North Carolina, where he was married to a woman named Eliza. They had a daughter, Bertha, but she did not survive.

After James death the 1930 census references James being born in the "Irish Free State" rather than "Ireland" based upon the country's liberation from the United Kingdom of Great Britain in 1922.

Judge James Shaw passed away at the age of 74 at 11 a.m. on Wednesday, May 30, 1906 in his Mt. Carroll home, which according to his obituary in the *Telegraph*, was quite a beautiful estate (having been designed by J. L. Silsbee of Chicago, IL).

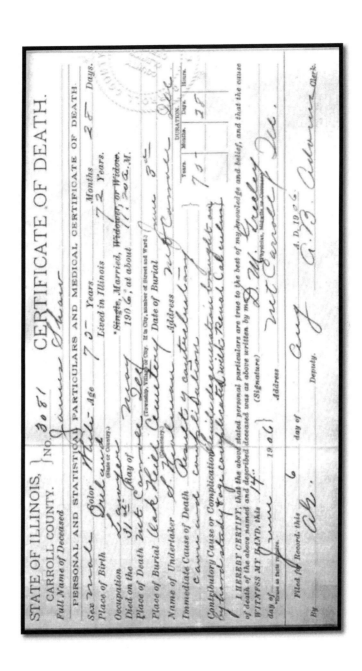

Death Certificate Courtesy of Carroll County

Judge James Shaw home Mount Carroll
National Registry of Historic Places
Photo by J. Thompson

According to the *Telegraph*, Judge Shaw's health had been failing for several years, which he spent in seclusion, and death was expected for many days as he had not left his home for three months. Many members of the Dixon Bar Association attended his funeral which took place in the Baptist church in Mr. Carroll on Sunday, June 3, 1906. Solomon was in Chicago at the time of his brother-in-law's passing but returned home for the funeral and interment at Oak Hill Cemetery.

The James Shaw home is of significant historic and architectural interest as it was built on commission by Joseph Lyman Silsbee, a prominent architect who worked in the Syracuse, Buffalo and Chicago areas. Silsbee was born in 1848 at Salem, Massachusetts and graduated from Exeter and Harvard Colleges.

He also attended the Massachusetts Institute of Technology in 1870, the year the architectural program was founded and coincidentally the first school to focus on architecture in the United States.

(Information Credit: Austin M. Fox "Dog on a High-Pitched Roof: The Question of Silsbee in Buffalo.")

Silsbee also designed the Solomon Hicks and Katherine Shaw Bethea home at 312 S. Ottawa Ave. in Dixon, IL and two homes in nearby Polo. The connection between Shaw, Silsbee and Bethea most likely occurred at the University Club in Chicago, as both judges and the architect, who opened an office in Chicago in 1886, were members. The club, lavish and exclusively discerning in its membership was a place where successful educated men could congregate, socialize and do business.

It is easy to imagine the three men happening upon one another, possibly over a fine cigar, and striking up a conversation in regard to vocation. Perhaps in the library or over dinner, Shaw and Bethea discussed their plans of building homes with Silsbee, who was noted as a fine architect with a flair for drawing. Conceivably, Silsbee may have taken a pencil from his breast pocket and made a few quick sketches for the men, who both, with little or no pause, hired him as the builder of their new homes.

Silsbee, although he produced many beautiful homes and designed the notable Lincoln Park Conservatory in Chicago, is also known as the first employer and mentor to Frank Lloyd Wright, the most prominent American architect in history. Wright even included a complimentary passage about Silsbee in his autobiography.

"Silsbee could draw with amazing ease. He drew with soft, deep black lead-pencil strokes and he would make remarkable freehand sketches of that type of dwelling peculiarly his own at the time. His superior talent in design had made him respected in Chicago. His work was a picturesque combination of gable, turret and hip, with broad porches, quietly domestic and gracefully picturesque. A contrast to the awkward stupidities and brutalities of the period elsewhere."

From "Frank Lloyd Wright Collected Writings, Vol. 2: Including an Autobiography, 1930-1932" [1992] Rizzoli International Publications (November 15, 1992) Edited by Bruce Brooks Pfeiffer.

Silsbee received the 1894 Peabody Medal from the Franklin Institute for his innovative design of the *moving sidewalk*, showcased at the 1893 World's Columbian Exhibition in Chicago.

Joseph L. Silsbee Photo – Christopher Payne

The Rest of the Boys:
Samuel Jr., Archibald, William and Timothy

The second eldest son, William, was born around 1835 in Cass County, Illinois. He attended school in Lee County and in 1850, at the age of 16, was working as a farmer with his father. Between 1860 and 1870 he married a woman named Kate Lennon of Lee County, and continued farming in Prairieville, independently working a large portion of his father's land.

By 1880 he had relocated to Cameron, Missouri where he worked as a stock dealer and lived in a boarding house with his wife. He then moved his family to DeKalb County, and made his home in Grand River, MO, where he worked in the stock trade. He and Kate had one child after 1880, but according to the 1900 census the child did not survive. William, along with his other four brothers, served as a Union soldier in the Civil War.

William passed away on Tuesday, February 14, 1912 around the age of 77. He died while staying at the Hotel Florence in San Diego, California after a three-week illness. He was survived by his wife. It can be assumed that the couple was vacationing in California, having recently won a sum of $2,500 as a result of litigation over the Elizabeth and Mary Shaw Estate, just five weeks preceding his death.

The third eldest son, Archibald, was born in Cass County on January 14, 1839. He stayed on at the family farm helping his father work the land until 1868, when he moved to Olathe, Kansas and began work as a livestock merchant. Before leaving Illinois, he married Kate Holbrook of Lee County in December.

Together they had three children, Leon, Royal and Henry. Leon was born in 1871 and went on to great success in the newspaper industry in Montana, acting as the editor and manager of the *Billings Gazette*.

Royal was born in 1873, and died at the age of five.

Henry was born in 1881 and, according to *A History of Montana*, later went on to become a publicity agent for the Kansas City Grand Opera Company.

Archibald "Arch", as he was called, found his niche working in the livestock trade, having been extensively engaged in the business of working cattle while on the farm with his father as a young boy. In an 1874 collection of biographical sketches of the residents of Johnson County, Kansas, it was said of Arch that he became one of the top stock dealers, of both cattle and hogs as a direct result from implementing his patented cattle feeder:

"In the spring of '74, he at one time shipped 60 head of cattle that weighed in the St. Louis market, and [*sic*] average of 1,620 lbs.; these cattle fed themselves at one of his patent self-supplying corn cribs."

The letters patent, "Improvement in self-supplying cattle cribs," was filed on February 24, 1874, and his invention was highly regarded by Johnson County farmers, as the cribs allowed for the successful fattening of cattle while eliminating half of the labor for the farmer.

He also served as a member beginning in 1878, of the Kansas Legislature for two years, and was a member of the Board of Regents of the Asylum for the Deaf and Dumb, serving on the building committee and as Treasurer. Archibald passed away May

15, 1888. He had been suffering from a tumor of the kidney as mentioned in the *Telegraph* obituary. He traveled to Chicago for treatment a few months before his death where an unsuccessful operation was performed. He stayed a few weeks in Dixon resting with family before returning to Kansas. He was remembered as a man always generous with family and friends, hard-working and ambitious with a knack for public enterprise, as clearly seen in all his accomplishments.

Samuel's fourth son Timothy, mentioned earlier, was born around 1841 in Cass County. While attending Illinois College in Jacksonville he enlisted as a Private for the Company B, 10th infantry regiment on April 16, 1861. This was the first call for troops during the Civil War and he thus through circumstance enrolled as the first volunteer from Lee County. Sadly, he died just three months later on July 29 in Cairo, Illinois which was a supply depot and Union Military camp. He was the first from Lee County to die in the Civil War although attributed to Morgan County.

Samuel's fifth son was Samuel Johnson Shaw, who was born around 1843. He left the family farm around 1860, and he also enlisted for the Union as a Private sometime between 1864 and 1865. After the war he attended the New York Law School at Albany. He lived with his brother Archibald in 1870 and was also attending law school during that time at Olathe, Kansas.

Samuel J. went on to practice in the capacity of lawyer in the real estate business in Kansas City, Missouri. When Samuel first moved to Missouri in 1880 he boarded in the home of Charles and Mary Torquist, a family of Swedish immigrants working as tailors.

Samuel spent much of his life as a bachelor until sometime between 1910 and 1920, when he married a woman named Ella, who was 17 years younger. It was not a long marriage as she passed away on January 7, 1920, leaving Samuel a widower until his unfortunate death resulting from 3rd degree burns when his home caught fire on Sunday, January 19, 1930. He was the last of the immediate Shaw family members to pass away. As noted in his death certificate, none of his family members were known and he was buried in the Forest Hill Cemetery in Kansas City on January 25, 1930. Samuel also received a sum of $2,500 from his sisters' estate in 1912.

Death Certificate Courtesy of the Missouri State Archives

Katherine's sisters:
Elizabeth J. and Mary Anna

The sixth child born to Samuel and Mary was a girl, Elizabeth J. Shaw. She was born in June of 1844, and passed away in 1910 at the age of 66. She worked diligently in the formation of Dixon's hospital with her brother-in-law Solomon, together doing all they could to see Katherine's vision come to fruition.

Elizabeth lived on the family farm keeping house with her mother for many years until she moved to Dixon to pursue her active life in the community. Her father, Samuel Sr. passed away in 1891, and having no other ties to the farm, she and her sister, Mary Anna moved into a home on North Ottawa Avenue in Dixon.

Elizabeth was described as a woman of incredible intelligence and an influential citizen. Her obituary appeared on the front page of the *Telegraph* on December 31, 1910, and it made mention of her many accomplishments. She served as a director and officer on the hospital board, and, "due greatly to her wise and judicious counsel ... the hospital has been financially well managed."

She also anonymously contributed articles to the *Telegraph* regarding local matters, which were always well-written and praised according to her obituary. She championed many women's movements in the area, ranging from church, civic and club life. Much like her sister, Katherine, she was deeply moved to be a voice for the poor and needy; "her heart and hand were always open to those who needed her."

This quality was marked especially by the care she gave to her younger sister, Mary. By 1900, they lived together in the Ottawa Avenue home with two German immigrants, Lena A. Ruppe, who was employed as a servant, and L. Emil Ruppe, who was a capper at a milk factory, which was probably the early Coss Dairy. The reason for keeping a servant was probably due to the demands of her younger sister's condition.

The seventh child, Mary Anna Shaw was born around 1850. She was rarely mentioned in the local papers, and although there is no substantiating evidence that something was terribly wrong with her, from what few references were made, it can be surmised that she suffered greatly from some mental condition.

In the 1880 Lee County census, at the age of 25, Mary was marked as suffering from Dementia, which was then used as a sort of general term to describe an array of mental disorders. The term comes from Latin, translating to "irrationality." The most commonly reported symptoms include a regression from daily life and the progressive loss of brain function. As we understand dementia today, it is most closely associated with Alzheimer's disease, although throughout history is has also been associated with Schizophrenia, Pick's Disease and other disorders.

The term Dementia was most likely misused in describing whatever was wrong with Mary. She could have had Downs Syndrome or was born with Hydrocephalus, or "water on the brain," which caused damage resulting in her lowered mental ability. She could have suffered a fall, perhaps from a horse on the farm as a young girl, and that trauma could have caused some sort of brain dysfunction in later life.

The fact that Mary also suffered from some debilitating illness is another glimpse into Katherine's motivations to lay the foundation for the hospital. As a family of means, Solomon and Katherine, as well as her sister Elizabeth, no doubt realized that many people in the area did not have the financial ability to care for loved ones suffering from such ailments. The Estate, which will be discussed later, allowed for a "free bed," providing much needed care for persons unable to afford medical attention.

Mary passed away on September 19, 1910 at the age of 60. Her obituary in the *Telegraph* was very short, a marked change from the rest of her siblings:

"...her strength had been failing, but her death was as peaceful and beautiful as her life had been. With a childlike faith in her Heavenly Father she had been looking forward through years of sickness to the time when she should meet her Savior and loved ones."

The words describing her as "peaceful" and "childlike," lead one to believe she had regressed greatly in mental ability during the course of her life. In Elizabeth's obituary this is significantly reinforced:

"She [Elizabeth] had been for many years devoted to the care of her invalid sister, and when her sister after a long illness recently passed away, the survivor was left with health much broken down by her long watchful care over the one that was gone."

Elizabeth and Mary never married nor had any children. The entire estates [of Solomon, Elizabeth and Mary] were left to the hospital and various community organizations, which lead to a month-long litigation involving brothers Samuel and William.

All family information attributed to 1904 History of Lee County by A.C. Bardwell.

Katherine Campbell Shaw Bethea Ancestry*

Samuel Shaw— 1803-1891
     Married:
Mary Campbell Shaw— 1810-1897

     Children:

          Hon. James A. Shaw— 1832-1906

          William Shaw— 1835-1912

          Archibald Shaw— 1839-1888

          Timothy Shaw— 1841-1861

          Samuel J. Shaw Jr.— 1843-1930

          Elizabeth J. Shaw— 1844-1910

          Mary Anna Shaw— 1850-1910

          Katherine C. Shaw— 1855-1893

*   Birth/Death/Marriage records are incomplete
     Shaw ancestral dates shown are approximate.

Chapter 2

Relentless Envious Death:
Katherine Shaw Bethea's Battle
with Tuberculosis

"The Lord shall smite thee with consumption, and with a fever, and with an inflammation, and with an extreme burning, and with the sword, and with blasting, and with mildew; and they shall pursue thee until thou perish."

~ Deuteronomy 28:22

Katherine Shaw Bethea
Courtesy of the Loveland Museum Collection

And this was the reason that, long ago,
In his kingdom by the sea,
A wind blew out of a cloud by night
Chilling my Annabel Lee:
So that her high-born kinsmen came
And bore her away from me,
To shut her up in a sepulcher
In his kingdom by the sea.

~Edgar A. Poe: third stanza, Annabel Lee, 1849

Virginia Eliza Clemm Poe died at age 24 in 1847 of consumption.

Dr. Douglas Gracey of Dixon was Chairman of the Pulmonary Medicine Division at the Mayo Clinic and explained Katherine's tuberculosis for this biography: "TB is an infectious airborne disease spread by coughing, sneezing, laughing, talking or even singing and has been known throughout the world dating back to the ancient Egyptians. In the 18th through 20th centuries many people in urban areas were infected with TB. The primary infection is found in the lung and most people have the immune system to wall it off and essentially cure it. However, if the disease progresses it spreads to more lung, bone, and the renal and nervous systems. It is not easy to become infected with TB and usually requires prolonged exposure to someone with the disease."

There is no evidence that Solomon contracted TB from Katherine. Although he was long-exposed to the bacteria that cause tuberculosis, his immune system must have been strong enough to ward off infection resulting in active TB disease.

In the 1800's tuberculosis clinics, or sanitariums, as they were called, were set up around the country, mainly in the West due to the "thin" air, which at the time was thought to be the best course of treatment available because it appeared to help shrink the lesions in the lungs that hindered breathing. Katherine spent a large amount of her adult life out West in either Colorado or New Mexico due to her condition and during that time her visits home to Dixon usually received brief mention in the newspapers of the area.

In 1882, ten years before Katherine's death, Robert Koch isolated the tubercle bacillus, establishing that tuberculosis was an infectious disease; however no effective treatment became available for the disease until the second half of the 20th Century.

Dr. Robert Koch
Photo Courtesy of the National Library of Medicine

There were several treatment procedures available for people with tuberculosis, many unpleasant. One method was to inject air directly into the chest cavity. Another surgery performed on tuberculosis patients was called Thoracoplasty, in which ribs were removed with the intent to collapse a patient's diseased lung in the hope of letting it heal. It is unknown which, if any, of these various procedures were performed on Katherine. She most likely spent time in the mountains on bed rest as noted in the *Telegraph* for treatment of this terrible illness. Katherine may have shown a number of symptoms, and it must have been torture for Solomon to watch as his dear wife experienced constant fatigue, weight loss due to loss of appetite, a persistent cough, fever, night sweats and the most horrific, coughing up blood.

Katherine spent many summers and even long into the winter months, in Colorado Springs. This no doubt was a strain on the marriage and the reason behind Solomon's decision to relocate to Colorado in 1885 according to the March 28th edition of the *Amboy News.*

"Sol. Bethea has gone to Colorado to live the remainder of this earthly life. We hope the genial, kind-hearted attorney may live long to enjoy life."

During this year it is unknown just what course of treatments Katherine was undergoing, but in July of 1886 reports of the Bethea family began to show up again in the *Telegraph.*

One can only surmise that Solomon wanted the best for his wife and for her to be comfortable, and for this he was willing to give up everything he had worked so hard to accomplish in Dixon. In discerning what one can from reading of Katherine's character in newspapers, it can easily be assumed that she saw the greatness in the man she married and did not want him to forfeit his success for her comfort. This is probably the reason the couple returned to Lee County and Solomon successfully continued his political career in Illinois. Katherine's affliction was undoubtedly the driving force behind Solomon's commitment to bringing a first-rate hospital to the area, and naming it for his wife, as he felt helpless against her disease.

Her course of treatment most likely consisted of bed rest and perhaps an array of elixirs one could purchase off a traveling cure-all man or by sending money to purchase the medical quackery advertised in the local newspaper.

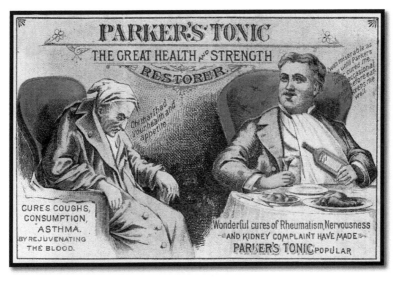

Typical ad for a cure at the time of Katherine's illness

Health care in the rural areas in the mid-late 1800's consisted mainly of home doctor visits by general practitioners, very few of them specializing in any one illness. The same doctor who visited the home to cure a cold or diagnose pneumonia was the same who delivered babies and saw patients through to their death. Katherine's bouts and remissions with tuberculosis were no doubt beyond the scope of a home visiting doctor, as physicians at the time were poorly educated or usually apprenticed under other poorly educated physicians.

Solomon and Katherine repeatedly made trips trying to improve her health even until her death. The second-to-last mention of one of these trips was made on March 12, 1892 (The *Amboy News*) when the couple left for Asheville, North Carolina.

Asheville was regarded as one of the best destinations for those wishing to heal from consumption, or "the white plague," as tuberculosis was so often referred. During this period in history, TB was the leading cause of death in the United States, and Ashville quickly became the nation's most famous destination for treatment of the disease. There is no way to be certain which boarding house or sanitarium Katherine spent time at due to the overwhelming number of sanatoria in and around the Buncombe County area between 1880 and 1930. What can be discerned from information available is that for the time, Katherine received the best available medical care in the nation for tuberculosis. The only people who were able to go to Asheville were undoubtedly affluent because the working class and others who had no money to spend on summer trips and train tickets were not able to afford treatment in such places.

The article, "Ashville: The Tuberculosis Era," published in the North Carolina Medical Journal by Irby Stephens, M.D., offers a wealth of information applicable to Katherine's experience.

The article mentions, almost exclusively, the "Old Winyah" sanitarium, one of the most prominent sanitaria of its day. The sanitarium was established by Dr. Karl Von Ruck in 1888 after he came to Ashville in 1886 with the express idea of starting his own sanitarium to conduct experimental work on tuberculosis. Winyah had no more than 60 beds and most of the other sanitaria were mere "boarding houses" in which people with tuberculosis, or "tuberculars," as they were called, were minimally cared for.

Winyah Sanitarium - Asheville
Photo Credit: The Special Collections Unit of the University of North Carolina at Charlotte Library, "Art Work of Scenes in North Carolina," 1895, Part 9

Judging by the time of Katherine's arrival in Ashville and her financial status, it can easily be assumed that this could very well be where she spent the final summer of her life. Solomon no doubt insisted she get medical attention from the finest, most renowned physicians, and for the time, Von Ruck fit the bill.

Dr. Karl Von Ruck.
Photo Credit: "Ashville: The Tuberculosis Era." Irby Stephens, M.D. Sept. 1985, North Carolina Medical Journal. Vol. 46, No. 9.

Von Ruck was considered among many as a controversial physician, aloof in his work but highly respected none-the-less. Born in Constantinople, he was the son of a German diplomat and was educated in Germany at both the University of Stuttgart, where he received a Bachelor of Science and the University of Tubing where he completed his Medical Degree. After coming to the United States he completed a second M.D. from the University of Michigan in 1879, coincidentally the same university Solomon graduated in 1872.

Von Ruck, who was expressly interested in tuberculosis throughout his time as a student, was present at the 1882 meeting in Berlin where Robert Koch announced his discovery of the tubercle bacillus. After this historic meeting, Von Ruck returned to the United States, closed his practice in Ohio and wholly devoted himself to the study of tuberculosis. At heart, Von Ruck was a scientist and in that vein he furthered his research by opening the Winyah Sanitarium, which was highly successful both financially and professionally.

The exact cost of attending the Winyah Sanitarium during the 1890's is unknown. However, during the Depression, the cost for a bed at Winyah was $50 a week, not including physician's fees. Any similar cost and given the extent of time Katherine spent in treatment leads to the assumption that Solomon spent substantial sums on his beloved wife's care, at least $700 a summer and almost certainly much more. In terms of today's healthcare expenses, the costs would be more than most could bear. The Betheas understood medical expense better than most.

One interesting course of TB treatment as suggested by Thomas Sydenham in 1742 was horseback riding. This may or may not have been prescribed to Katherine but as mentioned in the *Telegraph* countless times, she frequently rode horses for pleasure. Sydenham wrote, "the principal assistant in the cure of this disease is riding on horseback every day, insomuch that whoever has recourse to this exercise in order to his cure, need not be tied down to observe any rules in point of diet, nor be debarred any kind of solid or liquid ailment, as the cure depends wholly on exercise."

Also mentioned in Thomas M. Daniels's book, "Captain of Death: The Story of Tuberculosis," is that this equestrian recommendation was practiced for many decades. In fact, the famous English poet John Keats, approaching death from tuberculosis rode horses until his final days in 1820.

In a biography of Solomon "Hix" Bethea written by L.H. Jennings, Secretary to Alumni Affairs for the University of Michigan, it was said that both Solomon and Katherine enjoyed equestrian exercise, "and took much recreation in riding and driving, both were noted for fine horsemanship in saddle and as drivers."

Immediately following this mention of horseback riding however, Jennings went on to write, "Mrs. Bethea was not strong, and had frequently to seek a milder climate."

Solomon returned to Illinois in May, 1892 for the Congressional Convention held in Sterling and was selected as a delegate to the National Convention at Minneapolis. It is doubtful that Katherine accompanied him on this return trip home; she most likely stayed on at Ashville to see out the summer there.

One could assume the couple returned to Dixon sometime between August and September but the exact time can't be established. This was Katherine's final journey back to Dixon where she would spend her final days at home and in her mother and sisters' home on North Ottawa. Tuberculosis was no doubt in its final stages as Katherine neared the month of her death. The couple was mentioned in the January 5, 1893 edition of the *Amboy Journal* as having returned home from a long stay in Colorado Springs for Katherine's health. The blurb also said her health was improving, but then 77 days later her health failed completely.

Unfortunately, Solomon had also lost his father only weeks before Katherine's death. William Wilson Bethea passed away in February, 1893 at the age of 81.

For Katherine, tuberculosis had won the relentless and dreadful battle, and on Wednesday, March 22, 1893, "Kittie" Shaw, as she was playfully nicknamed from childhood, sweetheart to Solomon Bethea, passed away. Her funeral was held at the North Ottawa Avenue home (NW corner of North Ottawa Avenue and East Chamberlin Street) of her mother and sisters, Elizabeth and Mary Anna, and she was interred at Oakwood Cemetery in Dixon.

Photos taken at Oakwood Cemetery by the author

Katherine's obituary in the *Telegraph*, quite poetic in its reflection of this life cut short at the age of 38, reads as follows:

"RELENTLESS ENVIOUS DEATH

Firmly as we may urge and believe in the amiable philosophy that every thing in nature is for the best—that 'whatever is, is right"—that all is for the highest good, still when death lays its iron grasp upon one whose life work has only fairly commenced: one whose charms of thought and intellect shed pleasure and love in many homes, optimism seems of but slight consolation. The thought that death is cruel forces itself upon the mind and we are compelled for the nonce whether we will or not, to become pessimists. While this must be the thought of one who remembers the dead of whom we speak as a neighbor and a respected friend, how well can we understand the sorrow of the bereaved who have watched day by day, night after night, to behold the hours and minutes pass in hastening the dearest of earth on to that inevitable doom we all must meet.

With loving, faint, but brave farewell words upon those trembling lips; to watch death's cruel blast fading out those cheeks once flushed with health and graced with vigor, is indeed,

'That desolating thought which comes into man's happiest hours at home.'

But yesterday Kittie Shaw, the child chaste and sparkling as the morning dew, then the bright, accomplished and refined wife of Hon. S.H. Bethea, today comes cruel death and claims her as his own and she is in heaven.

In the death of Mrs. Katherine Shaw Bethea we have most truly illustrated the adage: 'A death bed's detector of the heart,' for never passed to the 'bourne from which no traveler returns,' a soul more brave in the last trying hour. Having her full faculties and realizing that she was at death's portal, she made full preparation for the event; giving discretions in minutest detail, not forgetting those she knew to be needy, and cheerfully speaking of death as though she were about to depart on a pleasant journey. There was no cant in her brave requests, for she gave all to understand that the nodding plumes were not appropriate for the dead, but only served to show the vanity of the living. The timid 'feels a thousand deaths but once.' The latter thought is recalled in the death of Mrs. Bethea: for never departed a braver soul. The King of terrors for her had no terror. Last night she met him with a smile as with his rude hand she was taken from loved ones and a happy home made desolate for she was its light and life and joy. Never died a braver heart: one that appeared more fully 'sustained and soothed by an unfaltering trust,' approaching death as she did,

> *Like one who draws the drapery of the couch about him and lies down to pleasant dreams.* "

Chapter 3

That Murder!

Solomon's Role in the Notorious Incident
at Bloody Gulch

"Every unpunished murder takes away something
from the security of every man's life."
~ Daniel Webster, Statesman, U.S. Senator and orator, 1782-1852

When James Penrose decided to investigate what was working his cattle into a frenzy near a bridge one mile south of Dixon on the morning of Friday, September 18, 1885, he stumbled upon the terrible scene of what would come to be known as the Bloody Gulch Murder, as well as someday coin the name of the road south of Dixon.

The *Telegraph* recorded the full incident on the front page, indicating in bold lettering, a simple and straight forward statement: **"SHOCKING MURDER."** This was the most brutal murder to occur in Dixon and all of the town's residents were shocked indeed, as if a terrible circus had come to town, disrupting the normal hustle and bustle of rural life in the pioneering town.

"Bloody Gulch" was really a creek and drainage way that had small bridges and crossings where rural road and farm traffic could make their way. Frederick Thiel's body was discovered below one of these crossings near what is today Dutch Road on September 18, 1885. Hot summer weather would have dried up the small creek, making stone and dirt available for a hurried burial.
Photo taken by the author

The 56-year-old farmer could only see one foot, as the rest of the body had been hastily buried, but the body appeared to have been dead for many days. Penrose gathered that the body had been there since at least the previous Saturday because that was when his cattle began to spook as they neared the bridge, something cattle will do upon catching the scent of blood.

Penrose was instantly repulsed by the discovery and ran distraught across the fields to where Wilbur Hill was plowing with a farmhand by the name of Dan Murphy. Penrose, barely able to speak, told the men there was a man under the bridge and that he was afraid to go back alone. The three men returned to the bridge and found the man covered partially by flagstones and what appeared to be fresh dirt. They removed some of the stones and then drove into Dixon and notified authorities.

It was soon discovered to be the body of one Fredrick Charley Thiel, 18, from Elgin, Illinois. The young man had been boarding at the Keystone House for several weeks and working as a traveling book agent, selling bibles, albums and other religious texts for John Gately & Co., of Chicago.

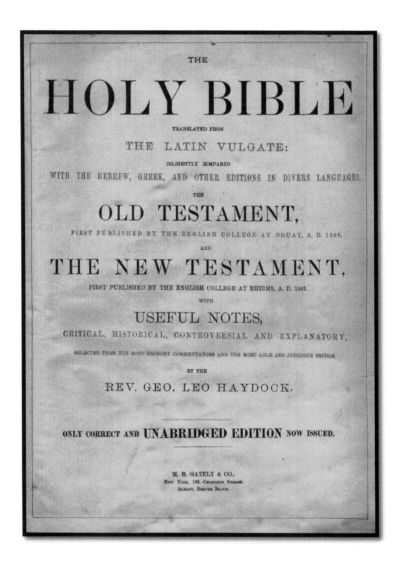

THE

HOLY BIBLE

TRANSLATED FROM

THE LATIN VULGATE:

DILIGENTLY COMPARED

WITH THE HEBREW, GREEK, AND OTHER EDITIONS IN DIVERS LANGUAGES.

THE

OLD TESTAMENT,

FIRST PUBLISHED BY THE ENGLISH COLLEGE AT DOUAY, A. D. 1609,

AND

THE NEW TESTAMENT,

FIRST PUBLISHED BY THE ENGLISH COLLEGE AT RHEIMS, A. D. 1582.

WITH

USEFUL NOTES,

CRITICAL, HISTORICAL, CONTROVERSIAL AND EXPLANATORY,

SELECTED FROM THE MOST EMINENT COMMENTATORS AND THE MOST ABLE AND JUDICIOUS CRITICS.

BY THE

REV. GEO. LEO HAYDOCK.

ONLY CORRECT AND **UNABRIDGED EDITION** NOW ISSUED.

M. R. GATELY & CO.,
NEW YORK, 195 CHAMBERS STREET.
ALBANY, BEATER BLOCK.

This is the frontispiece of a Bible similar to one Thiel would have been shopping around town. Though more information about Gately and Co. could not be located, religious texts available for purchase from a door-to-door salesman were often heavy leather-bound, beautifully designed books. They would have been a special purchase for a household, as their quality was much higher than bibles for sale at a general store or given from a local church.

When Marshall Woodyatt and several others arrived at the scene, they finished uncovering the body and took it to the courthouse where the coroner then made investigation of the body. Thiel, who was described as a small man of boyish appearance, had been left in the ravine, his throat violently cut ear to ear, in addition to having a hole in his head. Accounts noted Thiel lived as a boy with his parents in Elgin and had been a member of the Elgin band and played second chair b-flat cornet. He was last seen in Dixon on Saturday the 12th, and his landlady told authorities that he paid his rent in advance so she was concerned why he had not returned.

According to Lee County Coroner, Dr. Paine, Thiel's right hand had been lacerated clear across the palm as if grasping at the murderer's knife, what we would call today a defensive wound. The hole in his head was attributed to a three-pound stone found near the scene, covered in blood and hair. His head was covered in more than one dozen gashes; his face covered in bruises and cuts which left his eyes completely destroyed and maggots were well on their way to decomposing his face entirely. The fingernail on his right index finger had been torn out, and his blood and dirt-stained clothing indicated the man fought desperately for life.

A shallow grave indeed—
Where Thiel's body was discovered by Penrose just to the right of
the dark entrance to the culvert, his head facing south. Thiel was
found, viciously attacked and apparently dead for many days.
Photo by the author

Dixon authorities wasted no time in apprehending a suspect. The police made their way to Julius Lloyd's farm where they found Joseph Mosse, 21, hauling manure to the fields. The young man seemed not in the least bit disturbed with the news of his arrest. Mosse, a French Canadian who came to the United States from Canada eight years previous, was arrested on suspicion because he had been seen with Thiel before his disappearance as told by witnesses.

Marshall Woodyatt and other Dixon officers – circa 1907
Woodyatt (center) was 42 at the time of the Mosse murder case.
Photo courtesy of Dixon Police Department

The *Telegraph* arrived to interview Mosse Friday afternoon in the county jailhouse, but because Mosse spoke poor English, he told the paper he would tell them everything he knew, were he not afraid his words would be misunderstood and possibly misconstrued. Lacking much to quote directly, the *Telegraph* made report of Mosse's demeanor instead, stating that he did not appear like a person who was capable of committing such a crime. Mosse was below medium build, a young man of dark complexion with a small mustache. Weighing in at around one hundred twenty-five pounds, there appeared nothing vicious about him.

The main theory initially developed as the motive for the murder was theft. When authorities arrested Mosse they found in his possession what appeared to be a gold watch chain resembling the one owned by Thiel. Police said that when Mosse put his coat on he attempted to throw the chain into the weeds near the barn when Marshall Woodyatt caught his arm and retained the chain as evidence. Early reports marked the chain as the single most damning piece of evidence as to Mosse's guilt.

Upon further investigation it was not gold at all but a simple metal chain coated in a cheap gold-like finish, available for about a dime at any general store. Most any man unable to afford a gold chain would have the same one, but why Mosse would attempt to discard the chain if it were his and not Thiel's would go on to raise many uneasy questions. When Thiel's brother, John, was shown the chain he identified it as the one worn by his brother.

Thiel, being in the sales trade, was also said to carry the profits from his book sales on his person. Some witnesses said that Mosse told them Thiel was making a lot of money selling Bibles and that he was attempting to help Thiel by directing him to homes where he believed Thiel could make a sale.

Other witnesses said they saw Mosse walking down the lane carrying a spade the morning the body was discovered. Mosse denied this accusation as well. It was then brought to light that a spade was missing from the Spiller house at which Mosse stayed. When shown the spade believed to be the one used to cover the body, Willis Spiller could not identify it as the one missing from his barn because he remembered carving his initials into the handle.

There was a "common" large pocketknife found by the body that could only be partially identified by one of Rosbrook's livery men as belonging to Mosse. The men, who worked with Mosse and saw him every day, told the *Telegraph* they had noticed nothing out of sorts with the young man and had never suspected anything to be bothering Mosse or setting heavy on his conscience.

Rosbrook & Wasley Livery Stable
Photo courtesy of The Lee County Historical Society

Authorities made a more comprehensive search of Mosse's possessions once he arrived at the jailhouse and found a tintype of

Maggie Smith. A tintype was an early photographic process in which a photograph was covered in an enamel-like substance for durability. They also recovered a ring which Mosse said belonged to the girl. The two had been seeing one another for quite some time and the *Telegraph* was "informed" they had plans to wed and that Maggie was home planning the marriage.

While Mosse settled into his new home behind bars, another man by the name of Arthur Nettleton was indicted for murder and became his cellmate. The two were observed playing cards together almost every hour of the day, "apparently as chipper and happy as young men who are preparing for the dance." This constant playing of cards was no-doubt a way for Mosse to escape thoughts of what his future might hold. His card playing seemed to put him in a sort of hypnotic state, as noted by his reaction when Thiel's brother snuck into the jailhouse to confront the man who was accused of murdering his younger brother.

The man instantly became hysterical, begging the Deputy Sheriff to let him have a crack at Mosse. "Why did you not think of his poor mother when you killed him? Oh I shall never see my brother again!" Thiel's brother cried. "Let me cut his heart out!"

Mosse never said a word to the elder Thiel; in fact he did not even turn to face the man screaming murderous desires at him through the bars. Instead, he simply asked, "What is trump?" and "High or low, Jack?", deeply caught up in a game of "45" with Nettleton.

Just prior to the coroner's inquest on September 19th, Mosse's ordeal took a turn for the worse and public opinion began to weigh heavily against him, with a "thousand and one" rumors flying around town. Over 700 men, women and children crowded into the courtroom to view the inquest; one can only imagine what sort of impression this experience must have had on the children, as the details of the state of the body were so gruesome.

It was during this spectacle of an inquest that Solomon Bethea stepped forward to represent the young man. Solomon passed the bar exam in 1875 with great honors at the age of 22 after studying under Judge J.V. Eustace. Always the ambitious, compassionate lawyer, the 33-year-old Solomon then left the courthouse to visit Mosse in the jailhouse and inform him that he had counsel. A ten-year veteran in the business of law, working with the highly-regarded firm of Dixon and Bethea, Solomon knew the man had little money and took this duty on pro bono.

The *Telegraph* made use of Thomas Hood's poem, "The Dream of Eugene Aram," saying that the poem read as if the late Hood was witness to the murder. In mentioning a report of Mosse being seen hiding a shovel under his coat on the morning the body was discovered, the paper quoted,

"Merrily rose the lark, and shook

The dew-drops from its wing."

In regard to the body being only partially covered by dirt, as if hastily buried after the rain in order to keep it a "secret," the paper went on to quote,

"That earth refused to keep."

By quoting the Hood poem the story seemed to imply of Mosse that he went back to visit the scene of the crime.

"One stern tyrannic thought, that made

All other thoughts its slave:

Stronger and stronger every pulse

Did that temptation crave,

Still urging me to go and see

The Dead Man in his grave!"

Such sensational writing, which was perfectly acceptable during this period, undoubtedly created an unbelievable amount of excitement in Dixon. The jury at the inquest came back with the decision that Mosse be held until he would face the grand jury during the next session of the circuit court, as they believed him to be the guilty party. On the 26th, Mosse nervously entered a plea of "Not Guilty." Solomon made a motion to quash the indictment, which was denied.

While the jailhouse was crowding with men and young boys desiring a glimpse at Mosse, hollering out questions and allegations, the accused remained calm, despite the occasional nervous tremble attributed to the stress of the situation. The small town of Dixon was flooding with gossip, and the following day, **"THAT BRUTAL MURDER!"** was printed on the front page, followed by, "Probably The Right Man in Jail…"

Part 1: The Evidence

"While not enough evidence has yet been developed to fasten the guilt, 'without a doubt,' upon Mosse, still, so surely are circumstances coming to light that appear to point to him as the wretch, that we have no doubt of the final result."

-- The *Telegraph*, September 21, 1885.

Throughout the entire court proceedings, and in the course of the initial investigation, all of the evidence secured against Mosse was deemed circumstantial. By the 23rd of September, authorities and over one thousand citizens had been through the crime scene, combing the pasture for articles that might shed light on the great murder mystery.

A Broken Ball Club

Marshall Woodyatt discovered a broken piece of balustrade (vertical wood supporting a railing), which was later paired with its mate and identified as the club the Spiller boy used as a baseball bat. Authorities took no time in stating that this hard club made of black walnut was indeed used in the murder.

The Marshall reported that Mosse probably took the club from the Spiller home to carry out the vicious assault on Thiel; however, the area was frequently used by local boys to play baseball, and absent from the reporting is that the club could have simply been broken in a game of ball and left in the field. Thiel's body did have many bruises but there was no blood found on the club to indicate that it was used in the murder.

A young boy, Louie Dixon, said during the coroner's inquest that he saw the book agent with "another man" carrying a club under his arm on Saturday the 12th. Dixon identified Mosse as the man with the club among the other prisoners in the jailhouse.

A Common Chain

The watch chain was many times recorded in the paper as being the key to pinning guilt upon Mosse's head. The chain made of cheap materials, which could be bought at any dime store, was *surely* going to send Mosse to prison. The chain that he "attempted to throw into the weeds" would be the link in evidence securing a conviction.

Thiel's brother, John, who was partially deaf, identified the chain as belonging to his brother, who he had not seen in over a month, and could not recall seeing the chain in over two months. It is curious that John would have seen the chain two months previous when Fred was home visiting in Elgin, but not have seen his brother wearing the chain in August when he again made a home visit. During this time a man's pocket watch was very much a part of everyday attire, as was the chain securing it to a buttonhole in his vest.

During the inquest Dr. Paine told the court that he had made meticulous investigation of the chain taken from Mosse finding: "...two spots of blood, one on the end and the other on the bar which fastens into the button-hole. The examination was made with a microscope."

If it was in fact blood, it would have been over a week old. Blood typically dries, flakes, and probably would have dropped off the chain, so whether or not this was actually blood was under scrutiny, and examination by microscope was far from "scientific," although it was the best means possible at the time. Also worthy of consideration is that the cheap patina on the chain would also probably show signs of wear and tarnish at those exact locations; where it was affixed to the watch and where it was secured in a button-hole.

An instance where the chain was again identified as belonging to Thiel was when a man came from Elgin who said he repaired a watch chain for Thiel. The man told authorities that it was indeed his own work in soldering a broken link. The paper went on to say, "The false glitter of that thin plating over that bogus chain was, doubtless, the "saint-seducing gold" that assisted in charming the wicked brute into murdering his 'friend.'"

Was Mosse's attempt to discard the chain a sign of guilt? Was Marshall Woodyatt so determined to apprehend a suspect for fear of the town's population going into mass hysteria, concerned there was a *murderer on the loose* that the chain story was a fabrication? Or was the "bloody" chain a true piece of evidence marking Mosse as the terrible murderer?

A Spade

The spade would turn up much controversy in the weeks leading up to and during the opening trial on January 16, 1886. Several people reported seeing a man with a spade, some identified Mosse as the man with the spade, while others could not. Mosse denied even having a spade that morning.

When Woodyatt asked Mosse what he did with the spade, Mosse replied, "What spade?"

"The spade you carried with you when you came from Dixon this morning."

"I did not have any spade."

"You were seen to have a spade."

"No sir, I had no spade," Mosse denied the accusation completely.

A woman by the name of Mary Barr told authorities that she had met Mosse on the road that morning and walked with him for a while. She said she knew him personally and that he did in fact have a spade. Mathias Levan also met the two and recalled seeing a spade, although he could not identify the man as Mosse. Nicholas Mossholder, from south Dixon, limped to the stand, having been shot through the thigh at "Buzzards Roost" battle in the Civil War. He said he saw a man carrying a spade walking with a young woman. He identified Mary Barr as the woman he saw, but went on to say, "Have not seen the man since."

Once again, during the opening remarks given by the prosecution, the spade was identified as belonging to Willis Spiller, although previously the man himself did not claim it to be his own. The prosecution went on to state, "but that did not matter."

Mary Barr said she left Mosse at a crossroad located 10 rods, approximately 165 feet, from the culvert. Mosse went west toward where the body was found and Mary returned home to prepare Mrs. Seybert's children for school. Mosse was met by the children on the road approximately 15 minutes later, where they and a young teacher, Miss. Forsyth, said they thought they saw him putting something into a hedge at the side of the road, and that he no longer was carrying a spade. Woodyatt told the court that a spade was recovered in the hedge.

A Golden Ring

On September 23rd the "most damaging piece of evidence" quickly changed when a gold ring was discovered at the crime scene. The newspaper reported the ring, "was probably worn by the murderer and lost in the struggle incident to the killing of his poor victim." It is very curious that a man already in possession of the real thing, a true gold ring, would steal a cheap watch chain. It was reported that the ring was borrowed, and that the owner fully recognized it. Woodyatt reported that the ring was 16 carat gold and had on it an enameled cross. When the ring was shown to Maggie Smith she identified it as the one she loaned Mosse, but later in the trial this would change. She had also loaned it to Frank Spiller, who recognized it as well.

The ring was discovered five days after the body, and, "It is not only very remarkable that it was found at all, but it appears almost a miracle that it was not, before it was discovered, trampled into the ground by the hundreds—and we might say thousands— of people who have visited the fatal grounds since Saturday."

The *Telegraph* made note that some people found this discovery so remarkable that they considered it a suspicious circumstance, possibly proving that someone other than Mosse was the murderer. This theory was quickly snuffed out when Marshall Woodyatt reported to have picked it up himself after the initial discovery by Penrose while combing the grounds.

Apparently Woodyatt was doing such a diligent job as detective that this unearthing was of no consequence. "...this suggestion is slimsy...Officer Woodyatt has worked up the case in a most complete manner..."

And what of the ring found in Mosse's pocket when he was first brought to the jailhouse? Perhaps it was the same ring, mysteriously turning up in two places at once, or perhaps it could lead the investigation in an entirely different direction altogether.

"As the boa constrictor tightens its grip upon its victim so do the concatenation of circumstances that are developed each day and each hour slowly but surely form a chain of facts which appear to coil about the man Mosse and point unerringly to him as the fiend who committed the diabolical murder."

-- The *Telegraph*, September 21, 1885

All of the evidence was deemed circumstantial and a simple fact is that countless people have been convicted solely by circumstantial evidence alone. The real question was how the evidence would be viewed by the jury, and whether or not they believed it strong enough to convict the man beyond a reasonable doubt. The *Telegraph* reported rumors of other evidence: a bloody lap robe from one of the livery's carriages, something about "sleeve buttons," a night ride in a two-horse buggy with a third party, and "many other rumors that we might mention, have no foundation in fact."

As the trial would unfold, the evidence, as well as witness accounts would come under fire; the crowded court room echoed with contradicting accounts from September 12th through the 18th of 1885. It would be Solomon Bethea's task to try and make sense of it all, standing beside the man who Dixon's residents did not know whether to support or crucify.

On October 10, 1885 Solomon filed an affidavit for a change of venue, as he firmly believed Mosse would not receive a fair and impartial trial in Lee County. The prosecuting attorney filed in opposition, and sure enough, the trial was put on the Lee County Circuit Court docket.

A Murder Sideshow: "Running the Gulch"

While the news of the murder was traveling fast among Dixon residents, forcing some to retreat indoors and talk late into the night about that terrible scene south of town, it was also causing excitement of a much different sort. The young men of town saw the murder scene as a challenge—a daring place to exhibit their courage, the perfect location for a test of will and manliness.

A group of young boys challenged a local barkeep, William Plien to visit "bloody gulch," picking him as a coward, but the story, as told in the *Telegraph* fourteen days after the terrible murder, painted Plien as anything but.

Adding incentive to the proposed challenge, the boys bet Plien five dollars that he would not carry through with a midnight visit to the troubled pasture and ravine just outside of town. "William took the bet with the alacrity with which a trout takes the fly on the eager angler's hook…" The five dollars, having the purchasing power of over $100 today, meant Plien had no choice but to throw any apprehension aside and bravely answer the intrepid dare.

"When graveyards yawn," around the hour of midnight, Plien was instructed to cross the bridge which had previously been the roof over Thiel's corpse. The boys all required proof that Plien actually visited the haunted place and told him, for assurance that he performed the duty, he carry an empty beer keg in his buggy and leave it at the bridge.

Plien then parted ways with the boys, the German blood in his veins pumping harder than it had ever in his life, and began the most fearful ride of his life. As the young man neared the gulch, "visions of goblins dawned and ghostly spectres [*sic*] seemed to pass through his mind." He tightened his grip on the reigns, so much so that courage seemed to ooze out of his fingertips, and as he got closer to the site, he put whip to his horse and was nearly flying over the prairie road.

The newspaper likened Plien's ride to that of Tam O'Shanter, a character in a poem by Robert Burns. O'Shanter takes a night ride on his horse, a mare by the name of Meg, and while on this ride he stops by a pub and gets quite intoxicated. When he continues his ride he goes through a part of the forest that is said to be haunted, and in his drunken state he sees witches, goblins and many unnatural things in the night.

But Plien's journey produced a different result, and the paper made mention regarding alcohol for courage, "William had not, we believe, the starter which Tam had enjoyed." A

70

contemporary engraving depicting O'Shanter's ordeal may be very close to what Plien had envisioned as he approached the bridge, pushing his horse faster and faster down the lane.

"Tam O'Shanter and Souter Johnny." Engraving by George Wilmont Bonner London: Marsh and Miller, 1830. First edition, Illustrated by Thomas Landseer

Plien spoke of his blood nearly freezing up as the bridge came into sight under the still-vivid light of the full moon on the 24th. (U.S. Navy Observatory Website) His hair stood on end like, "quills upon the fritful [*sic*] (fretful) porcupine," and he felt as though he was entering the valley of the shadow of death. He drove his horse on, cracking the whip again and again across its old withers, and flew over the bridge.

He did not forget to lighten his load as proof to collect his five-dollar prize, and hoisted the empty keg overboard. He could not even muster the nerve to stop and place it on the bridge, nor did he look back after he had cast the wooden barrel off his rig. The keg was found the next morning on the road. The boys deemed it close enough to the bridge, and told Plien he had won the bet easily, and handed over the prize.

For this amazing exhibition of nerve, William was looked upon as a hero around town after the astonishing ride, and, "...his saloon was full of an extra run of customers who are all anxious to know how in the world he could have the nerve to run Murder's Lane and Bloody Gulch in the dead hour of night."

Part 2: The Proceedings

"...there came a strange coincidence which is, that within two weeks after Thiel's body was discovered here, another agent for the same book establishment that Thiel represented, was killed in a similar manner and the murderer is not discovered."

-- The *Telegraph*, December 30, 1885

Nearly three months after Joseph Mosse was indicted for the murder of Fredrick Thiel, the newspaper announced the jury selection was slated to commence on January 8, 1886. "...we might say that the mystery which surrounds the case makes it one of the most remarkable tried in this country."

In the three months Mosse was behind bars, rumors continued, but a strange shift in opinion occurred. Dixon's residents had time to reconsider not only the evidence, but also the character of the young man, and it seemed that public opinion toward Mosse was becoming favorable, "and all are anxious to hear the other side before condemning him."

On top of this change in public opinion, jail guards were speaking out as well on behalf of Mosse. They spoke highly of the young man, saying without hesitation that they never had a more quiet and gentlemanly prisoner. While in jail, Mosse was employed in the neighborhood and all of the men he worked for spoke of him as an honest, thoughtful, hard-working, good-hearted young man. All of the people he had befriended while staying at Spiller's and working at Rosbrook's wrote letters of praise on his behalf to the editors of the *Telegraph*.

The Mosse trial was officially called to order on Wednesday, December 31st at 5:00 p.m. Attorney Charles Morrison, assisted by Judge Farrand, would represent the prosecution for the people, and Solomon Hicks Bethea appeared for the defendant. As Solomon sat in the chilly courthouse, a single wood-burning stove in the corner to his right, he quietly waited for the sheriff to bring in Mosse.

When the young man arrived he sat next to Solomon, and despite his generally calm demeanor, Mosse was clearly thinking very hard about the events in the days ahead of him. Frequently catching a concerned eye with Solomon, Mosse looked to the attorney as his only true friend in the world.

"He has a neat, we might say, tidy appearance, and taking him all-in-all, is about the last person in all the crowded court room that a stranger would select for a murderer, were it not perhaps for the sad, earnest, anxious look that constantly stamps his every feature at all times."

-- The *Telegraph*

Mosse was dressed in a plain black suit, the same one he had prior to his arrest. He had taken care to make himself as neat and presentable as possible, parting his light brown, neatly cut hair a little to the side. He also had a mustache, dark auburn in color, just long enough for him to occasionally twist the ends in his fingers. His strong jaw and broad forehead were lightly covered with pimples, a true showing of his young age and the stress he had endured since his arrest; despite this, Mosse was looked-upon as a very handsome man. As the jury selection commenced, his kind hazel eyes moved from attorney to attorney, occasionally directing a sincere glance to Judge William Brown.

From this point forward his eyes stayed fixed on the candidates for jury. The simple young man studied each juryman, and during the next fifteen days, over 100 would be summoned, examined, and turned away, most because they did not believe in capital punishment. Mosse watched solemnly as they left the courtroom, knowing full-well that the jury would be made of men unmoved by the idea of putting a man to death, unmoved by the thought of sending a quiet, Canadian-born boy to his grave.

At 10:40 a.m. on January 16, 1886, the final juror was accepted. Half of the jury was comprised of Amboy residents, the other half consisted of from two from Nelson, and one from Nachusa, South Dixon and Sublette. The trial could officially begin, and the prosecution submitted a list of 87 witnesses, while Solomon submitted a list of about 50; with a potential 137 witnesses to take the stand, not one of which actually saw the crime committed, it undeniably would prove to be one of the most impressive trials to-date in the State of Illinois.

Opening Remarks: The Prosecution

Prosecuting Attorney Morrison began his opening address to the jury by pointing out the relationship between Mosse and Thiel. In his first few words, Morrison said, "On the afternoon of the supposed time of the murder, at about three o'clock, Mosse called Thiel from the Keystone House porch, and they had a talk in the street, separated, and soon after Thiel left the hotel where he boarded and was not seen alive after that afternoon."

Morrison devoted his entire opening remarks to refreshing the court of all the various evidence and brashly stating that it would, without a doubt, mark Mosse as the heartless murderer. Morrison also commented on new matters that had previously not come out in the papers, such as when authorities arrived to arrest Mosse, Julius Lloyd told them that Mosse said to him, "I have a mind to tell the truth." Lloyd then put a hand on Mosse's shoulder and said, "Tell them all you know, this is a serious matter."

Another incident not reported during the initial arrest was that Woodyatt forced Mosse to go view the body. Since Woodyatt knew that Mosse and Thiel were acquaintances, he asked Mosse to identify the body as well, because he, "desired to hear what he would say about the affair." Morrison stated that Mosse did not want to go to the crime scene, that he outright refused to go, but was taken there anyway. "I don't want to look at the murdered boy," Mosse said.

Morrison went on to say that Joseph was, "very much excited while there." In using the word excited, it seemed as though Mosse could have been nervous or guilt-stricken, perhaps even fidgety. It could also mean merely that just like anyone viewing a horribly mutilated body; he was completely sickened and wanted to get as far away from it as possible. The decaying corpse of a young man he had a few friendly chats with outside the boarding house would surely upset Mosse, just as it would anyone else for that matter.

Another curious comment made by 12-year-old Louie Dixon was also mentioned in Morrison's opening. At approximately 3:45, not even a half-hour after Mosse and Thiel had an uneventful talk outside the Keystone House and split ways, Louie, Mrs. Sherwood Dixon and James Curran claimed to have seen the two, Mosse with a club in his hand, walking down the road toward where the body was found.

"Wonder if he is going to kill that other fellow?" Louie reportedly said.

The remark was taken as anything but boyish by the reading public. It's strange this comment came out so long after the

76

murder occurred. It's also strange that even though Louie had apparently said those exact words, claiming he knew exactly who the two young men were, that when Thiel was reported missing, and days before the body was discovered, he never came forward with the information.

It is also noteworthy that no one saw the men rejoin after outside the Keystone House, located on First Street. The site of the murder was a mile and three-quarters from the hotel, making it a very fast walk through, and then out of, town. The walk would have taken approximately 25-30 minutes at least and how much extra time would it have taken, and how far out of the way would it have been to pick up the ball club from Spiller's place?

With these questions and theories set in the mind of the jury, Solomon Bethea could begin his opening remarks, address all of Morrison's statements, as well as make an argument for the defense.

The Defense Opens – Solomon Bethea

"May it please the court—Gentleman of the jury: It is with more than ordinary embarrassment that I rise before you." In this instance the use of the word "embarrassment" is archaic, and should not be construed as Solomon Bethea stating he had any feelings which we associate today with the word. In choosing this word, Solomon meant that the case was beyond normal complications and presented great difficulties. Solomon, throughout his opening remarks, frequently interjected the importance of examining circumstantial evidence, and that the jury had a great duty before them in determining Mosses' innocence or guilt.

Solomon also paid special attention to the events which occurred after the discovery of the body and the arrest.

"…I address you in this young man's behalf. For three months the newspapers of the county, the scandal mongers of the county and those who live upon rumor and gossip, have had it over and over in their mouths as to what they understood to be the evidence of the case…you have here before you a man without a friend, without money, without home. You have a man who in his early youth lost his mother; who from childhood has been compelled to earn his living, and has done so honestly. A man who never before was charged with any wrong thing in this world."

Solomon also repeated the evidence to the jury, paying special attention to the discrepancies in securing the evidence, as well as the integrity of the evidence itself. He made every effort to firmly place the word "circumstantial" in the mind of the jury and to make the tie between that fact and the grave task of being in charge of a man's life.

"It will appear that there were thousands of people examining these premises from the day of the arrest, the 18th of September, until a week afterwards. The grounds were examined by nearly everyone in this town from judges of the courts down to small children, and no human being could find the ring or could find the club there until after the newspapers had announced that a ring might be found and that if it was found it would be evidence against the young man, and after that there was sufficient opportunity to arrange the circumstances and place the criminating articles there."

Solomon's attention to detail and vast understanding of law was expertly demonstrated when he quoted several cases, one of which was argued by Abraham Lincoln, to the jury which resulted in men being convicted of murders they did not commit on circumstantial evidence alone, years later to be acquitted. He went on to state the risk in relying exclusively on human accounts of events.

"I want to say to you that this is the most dangerous testimony in the world. One person cannot recognize another merely by looking through a window and be absolutely sure that he is the person they think…By the testimony of boys, the evidence of children, the evidence of people who did not know him, they talk about hanging on such testimony."

The Spillers, where Mosse boarded, said that he went to town after breakfast and returned back home between half-past three and four o'clock. He then changed his clothes and went back downtown to pick up some goods he purchased and returned to the Spillers before six p.m. to have dinner on the day of the murder. Solomon made note of this to show the improbability of Mosse committing the murder in this time frame.

He also addressed the instance of Woodyatt forcing Mosse to view the body.

"No man would want to look at anything of that kind, and he had no feelings because he did not want to look at blood or dead people."

Solomon again urged the jury to take their responsibility as a very serious matter, to rid their minds of anything they had read in the papers or heard on the street, and look at the evidence alone and Joseph's integrity, in deciding his fate. He reminded them that every man must be presumed innocent until proven guilty, and if they had any practical doubt in their mind that Mosse committed the crime, it was their duty to set him free of all charges.

Solomon closed by saying, "Remember, no living person can raise his hand against him and say, 'you are the guilty man.' No human being knows that, unless perhaps it be himself."

Part 3: The Trial - Witnesses for the Prosecution

The Brother

Frank Thiel's older brother, John T. was the first witness called by Morrison to the stand. He was asked by Morrison, who had to raise his voice in order for John to hear him, to identify a watch chain, which he did. He remarked that it looked like blood stains on the chain. Solomon did not wish to cross-examine, so Judge Brown asked him to step down. As John passed Mosse on the way back to his seat, he looked at Joseph in a very searching manner, as if hoping something in his hazel eyes would give way to the truth. He didn't have a look of anger toward Mosse, and quietly passed him by.

The Doctor

Doctor Paine was then called to the stand; the 38 year old physician simply recounted the condition of Thiel's body, but noted that he theorized Thiel had been beaten and stabbed and left in the culvert, and that the killer returned later, and upon finding him still alive, slit his throat.

When Solomon cross-examined Dr. Paine, he asked him what experience he had with making these sorts of observations. The doctor said he had none, that he had never before seen anything of the nature of the murdered boy. The doctor also said it was hard to determine if the stains on Mosse's clothing were blood, and furthermore, even if it were animal or human. Mosse, being a farm laborer often killed and plucked chickens, and on one occasion was in charge of killing a mad dog. Probably the most striking statement the doctor said when presented with the watch chain was, "It is difficult to distinguish blood on metals from rust."

Many of these statements differed from those he had made three months prior during the inquest. Perhaps in putting his hand on the Bible, a more reserved, conscientious answer came from his lips. This testimony left all the blood evidence thin at best, and when re-directed he was asked about the knife. He testified that it was a very large, common, cheap pocket knife. He said he found blood on the wooden-handled knife, which was said to have been recovered from the crime scene. He also remarked that the blade was two inches long and rusty, but sharp. The doctor said the blade appeared to have rusted significantly since he first examined it, which is a bit curious how that would occur.

81

The Sister

Barbara Thiel, Frank's older sister by eight years who worked in a watch factory in Elgin, was then called to the stand. She was asked to make identification of the watch chain and she said it belonged to her brother. "The defense here admitted that the chain was worn here by Thiel." This statement, which was in parenthesis in the newspaper, could mean that Mosse admitted to be in possession of Thiel's chain, though it could have been a gift, loaned, traded, or at worst, stolen from the body.

The Others

Next, Godfrey Mann was called to the stand. He was employed as a dial maker at the Elgin watch factory, probably the same one where Barbara kept employment. He testified that he knew Thiel and had done some soldering work on the chain and recognized it as his own craftsmanship.

Mrs. Brautigam, keeper of the Keystone House on First Street where Thiel was staying, said Mosse came to the hotel and, "asked to see the book agent." She testified that she had seen Thiel wear a watch chain but could not identify the one presented as evidence.

When cross-examined by Solomon, Brautigam said Thiel arrived with about $75 worth of bibles, albums and prayer books and that he was out every day selling books. She also said that a fellow book agent called once for Thiel, but did not know his name. She also testified that, "Thiel made acquaintances with the two men who were blacked up and sang on the street for the man selling electric belts."

Mrs. Brautigam's daughter, Clara, was then called. She remembered sitting on the porch of the Keystone House with Thiel the day of his disappearance, and that she last saw him on the corner of Peoria and First Streets, but that he was alone.

When Solomon began his questioning, Clara said she assumed Thiel went off with the black-faced singers and that she had not told anyone this before. The men would have probably been traveling minstrels, living a sort of gypsy lifestyle, making money by performing on the streets, or in this instance, for the street peddler.

As an aside, the electric belt was quite an odd contraption, but popular for men seeking to lose pounds around the waist. It is no surprise many people were injured as a result from using the belts. It's an interesting visual to think about Thiel standing around an electric belt peddler, speaking with two black-faced nomads, with a huge poster, resembling this illustration from the 1902 Sears and Roebuck catalog hanging in the background.

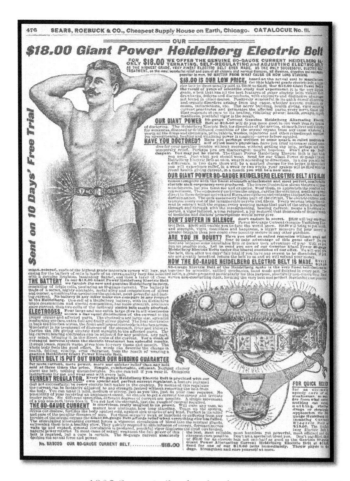

1902 Sears & Roebuck advertisement illustration

George Leonard, a barber, who owned a shop on First Street, was sworn next; he remarked that he'd seen Thiel and Mosse on several occasions at the Keystone House, the last occasion being the afternoon of Thiel's disappearance. He also reported the boys talking for ten or fifteen minutes and then parting ways. At some point in his testimony, Leonard made a statement as to his opinion of the guilty person. Bethea cross-examined after this statement and Leonard said sharply that he was, "no dog-oned liar." Since the statement was stricken from the record, it is unknown who he thought was the guilty party, but it seems as though he thought it was Mosse.

A Mrs. Lawrence McDonald was then called; she lived near the Chicago and North-Western depot, and said she saw Thiel with someone on the day of the murder, but could not say it was Mosse.

Another woman, Mary Curran reported to have seen Mosse with Thiel that afternoon. When cross-examined by Solomon, he wanted to know how she knew it was Mosse. She said she recognized him, but Solomon then asked her what her vantage point was. She said the house was 50 feet from the road, that she was inside and there was a fence and trees with leaves on them in her field of vision.

At this point the young Louie Dixon was called. He was asked about the club Mosse was reported to have been seen carrying with him on his walk with Thiel. He kept referring to it as a "stick." He told Solomon that when Woodyatt showed him the broken club recovered from the scene that he, "Never saw any club that looked like that." It was also made known that he talked about the murder with his mother first and then with all the boys at school.

Another boy, Jas. Curran, aged 16 was called. He told the court that he had seen Mosse with Thiel, and when asked by Solomon, "What sort of a person is the person with Thiel?" Curran said, "There he is now," gesturing toward Mosse. The boy could not however, describe what Thiel looked like, or anyone else for that matter, who happened to be on the road that day, and also said he was at least 55 yards from the men when he saw them.

Next, a Chas. Knoble was sworn. He told the court that Mosse lived at his house with Maggie Smith for eight months, October of 1884 through May of 1885. When shown the infamous ring, he said it resembled the one Maggie wore. Still, there was no mention which ring was used as evidence. Was it a ring found on Mosse? Was it a ring found later by Marshall Woodyatt? Was it a ring missed in all the searching of the area by the Gulch?

In the following hours and days, the prosecution was calling witnesses, and Solomon Bethea was in charge of picking the evidence apart piece by piece. In the end, over 50 witnesses were called to the stand, each trying to recollect the times, places, dates and various objects they could remember in regard to Thiel and Mosse. It was a parade of memories, some distinct, some not. Many utterances such as, "I'm not sure," and "I don't recall," and "Haven't seen the man since," were said on the witness stand.

There was a lot of talk about the ring, and in-fact when Maggie Smith was called to the stand, she was asked to put it on. In doing so, she said, "It don't seem to fit like the ring she [I] gave Mosse." Attorney Morrison then re-directed, asking if the size of her finger could have changed. "[I] don't know that there is any difference in [my] finger now than last September."

The questioning went around and around in regard to the integrity of the evidence. The knife came into question on a few occasions, with Willis Spiller making note of the curious rust that had appeared on it when it was shown in court.

There were also differing accounts in regard to the club, which was identified by a six-year-old boy as being the one they played baseball with in the fields. The spade came into question almost constantly, one witness re-calling Mosse using it, or something like it, as a walking cane. The spade was never solidly identified by anyone; questions of it being rusty or not, caked in mud or not, having a splintered handle or not: these were all matters brought up during the testimonies. The final inventory of evidence as brought by the people was Mosse's coat and pants, the stone found at the scene, the stick, or club, the spade and photographs.

John Plien was called last (before E.M. McCune, a photographer, who verified photos of the scene and the final submittal of evidence), this being a smart move on the part of the prosecution, because he lived at the 'Brewery.' The questions asked of Plien were simply when and where he last saw Mosse. His answer was that it happened to be Wednesday evening before the arrest at Louie Stephan's saloon, and a few times earlier in the week. This technique was probably employed in the final questioning for a very distinct purpose: to associate Mosse with the consumption of alcohol. Plien said that Mosse asked him for a pony of beer, and later a pail of beer to take to the country, "for his health." The jury listened and heard it all. The People rested.

Part 4: Solomon Hicks Bethea for the Defense

"You never really understand a person until you consider things from his point of view—until you climb into his skin and walk around in it."
~ Atticus Finch, *To Kill a Mockingbird,* by Harper Lee, 1960

Solomon opened his defense with strong scrutiny in regard to the pocket knife recovered at the scene. He first called Joseph W. Cowley, who, "sells Yankee notions" throughout the area. One such item he sold dealers was cigars, which were accompanied by 'prize packages,' which included one and a half dozen knives identical to the one in question. Per 1,000 cigars, 18 'prize' pocket knives were given to each local dealer. Dealers in Franklin Grove, Ashton and Dixon sold the cigars, and Solomon made firm note that there were at least 54 such knives floating around the area, and that Willis Spiller had won a knife himself.

When the trial spilled into the next day's paper, it was noted that it was coming to a close.

"The accused tells his story. He says he traded the tell-tale ring for the blood-stained chain. Took the spade to dig ditches, not graves."

Solomon then called Wallace Seibert to the stand, a man who owned land near the culvert. Seibert testified that he saw men working on the culvert when it was being built (to substantiate his vantage point), and that he remembered seeing two teams and a man pass by the culvert on the supposed day Thiel was killed.

Next a Mrs. Mont Flatt was called to the stand. She said she had seen the book agent walking with a man of very dark complexion on the same road a week before the murder. She testified that he had no mustache and that the defendant was certainly not the man she recalled traveling with Thiel. Her testimony turned theatrical when Morrison began his cross-examination. He asked Mrs. Flatt if the book agent had a mustache and she said she had not noticed because the darker man was so terrible looking, like a tramp. Morrison then robustly stepped in front of the witness and asked, "Does Mr. Bethea have a mustache?" To which she replied, she did not notice him. It is unclear if she was speaking of the man in question or if she was referring to not noticing if Solomon had a mustache.

Solomon then addressed the supposed blood stains on Mosse's pants. He called two surgeons who both testified that blood was nearly impossible to identify unless it was fresh, in which case, it could be identified by smell. He then called Peter Ramsy and his wife, who had employed Mosse as a brick maker the previous summer. They both re-counted the instance of Mosse killing a "mad" dog at their home. Mrs. Ramsy told the court that she had seen Mosse bring a club down on the dog's head and blood spurted out on his pants, but she could not say if they were the same pants in question.

Next, Solomon called Mrs. Spiller. She testified that she had done Mosse's laundry the Wednesday after the murder, and that she noticed no blood stains of any sort on his clothes. When cross-examined she said she had told her sister that the woolen shirt was very dirty, and apparently her sister suggested that it may have been blood. She then told the court that she asked Mosse to kill her cat previous to the washing, which he did. It was never mentioned why she made this strange request. Finally, she told the court that when she observed Thiel's watch chain it had a brightly colored stone charm on it, and she did not recognize the chain in question as Thiel's.

A few more witnesses were then called, all of the questioning of these was in regard to times and dates of "Mosse-sightings." The goal of this was to demonstrate to the jury just how confusing the times, dates and places in which Mosse was seen were to recall; one witness, Henry Evarts, even asked not to be questioned, as he felt he could not stake his testimony on his memory and that he was not, "apt to say anything that is not true."

The Defendant Testifies

Solomon then called Mosse to the stand and began his questioning in order to show the court who Mosse was as a person and demonstrate his general background. The *Telegraph* made note of the way questions were asked, and that Mosse spoke tolerable English, but that there were many words he did not understand. A humorous example of this occurred when Morrison asked him if he was a coward.

Mosse replied, "A Cow!"

"A coward; you are no coward?"

"I don't look like that, do I?"

"I mean you are not afraid?"

"I am not so afraid to run."

"I mean you are brave, are you not?"

"I don't understand."

Through the questioning, the court was told Mosse's life story so-to-speak. He was born in St. Thomas, Canada, and a year later his mother passed away. His father was a very poor farmer who sent Mosse to live with his aunt after the passing of his mother. He attended school while he lived with his aunt, not very far from his father, until he was 15 when he left for the United States. He first lived in Massachusetts for three years and then Indiana for a few months before coming to Dixon.

Solomon then began to ask Mosse about the murder itself. When handed the knife, Mosse said it was not his knife because the small blade was broken on his pocket knife. He testified that he and Thiel knew each other but that he did not go with him to the country to sell Bibles, and that he never had any trouble with the book agent. Mosse also testified he and Thiel traded the ring for the watch chain. It was at this point Morrison began his cross-examination.

Cross of Mosse and Others

Note: The following passages have been taken directly from the court transcript as printed in the Telegraph on Monday, January 25, 1886.

Morrison was particularly harsh when cross-examining Mosse; for example, he questioned Mosse six different times as to whether or not he lost his pocket knife while unloading hay for Johnny Hetler. Mosse explained every time that he simply remembered that being the last day he saw the knife. Mosse's answers to the questions were very straight-forward and matter-of-fact.

Morrison: "Did you ever look for it (the knife)?"

"No sir."

"You know where you lost it?"

"If I know where I had lost it I would go back and pick it up."

Morrison would ask Mosse the same question over and over again with intense frequency, hardly re-phrased, no doubt as a tactic to catch Mosse in a lie. His replies to many of the questions were, "I do not know," and "I do not remember."

After Mosse stepped down from the stand Mrs. Spiller was re-called. She was again asked about the club Woodyatt recovered from the scene, and testified again that she did not recognize it. Morrison then asked her if she did or did not tell her sister in passing that if she could clear Mosse by swearing to a lie she would be tempted to do it, which she said she believed she did. Solomon then asked her if she told her sister that because she believed Mosse to be absolutely innocent. Her answer, which was not printed in the paper, was ruled out of order by the court, and she stepped down.

Maggie Smith was then called to the stand. Maggie, at the young age of 19, was full-faced, "a healthy lass," and was very deliberate in her answers. The *Telegraph* reported that she spoke as if she were the only person in the courtroom. It was noted that one little slip of the tongue might condemn Mosse, which was why she was so deliberate in her remarks.

She had seen Mosse the day before the murder and recalled that he was at Spiller's place most of the day, only leaving to go into town for a few hours. He had returned to the house with a Bible around 1:00 p.m. and then went to the depot with Mr. and Mrs. Spiller around 4:00 and stayed in for supper and the evening.

Maggie then re-counted the day of the murder. She said she saw him at breakfast and she was picking chickens that afternoon and Mosse was helping her. After he departed from helping at 3:00, Maggie did not see him again until after 6:00 when he returned to Spiller's place, where he changed his clothes, combed his hair and sat in the kitchen shining his boots.

After Maggie stepped down, she took a different seat in the courtroom. Instead of returning to her previous seat, she sat near Mosse, something she had not done in the previous days. As she walked to her seat, a look of deep-sadness was fixed on her face; indicating a deep-running sorrow as observed by a *Telegraph* reporter.

Part 5: Closing

Prosecution

First to begin his closing remarks was R.S. Farrand, Morrison's assisting attorney. It was noted that Farrand had been ill during the previous three days of the trial and was weak. He told the court that he may not be able to speak long.

The first words to spill from Farrand's lips were in direct criticism of Solomon's defense.

"Mr. Bethea will take you to England, he will take you to Scotland, he will take you to Ireland, to get you away from this case... I ask you now, gentlemen, if this man [Mosse] is guilty, if he perpetuated this deed. I ask you not to look upon him here while he is on his good behavior but take him as he was then, see him as he was enticing that young man away and see him as he did it..."

He then went so far as to say that the jury was, "doomed to disappointment," in regard to Solomon being unable to "throw the penetrating light of explanation, at least, upon the evidence that surrounds this man." He then went on to quote Solomon's opening statement, when he communicated to the jury that the gravest task was upon their heads in deciding a man's fate.

"If you convict an innocent man you have committed a great wrong: if you let a guilty man go, you have committed just as great a wrong." Farrand went on to speak about the ring. He told the jury that Solomon did not comment on the ring until after an article ran in the *Telegraph* which stated countless people had been through the crime scene. It was only then, Farrand said, that Solomon told the jury Mosse had traded the ring for the chain.

"Mr. Bethea did not know when he began this trial, or if he did, kept it locked up in his own breast, that this man had ever traded that ring to Frank Thiel."

Farrand then addressed the jury directly, playing on their heartstrings as only a seasoned attorney knows how: "I ask you gentlemen to turn your thoughts to God and ask him to guide and direct you while Mr. Bethea speaks, that you may go home in your closet to your God and say that you have done your duty. Mosse was the first to say Thiel was going away; he did go away and never came back alive. He was seen with Mosse fifty minutes before the cattle were bellowing at the blood spilled ground."

He continued his speech by stating that nearly one dozen witnesses testified to have seen Mosse with Thiel there on the road that fateful Saturday. He also mentioned Mosse's responses to Morrison's questioning, in that he often said, "I do not understand the English language." However, he also said Mosse understood Morrison until, "he began to wind and twist him up."

Farrand concluded his speech by telling the jury to, "lift your hands to God and render a verdict, that when you meet your family, and the little ones are prattling on your knee, you can say to your children and wife: We have passed a week in the most solemn duties we have ever performed, but we saw the right in the presence of God, and the presence of each other, we performed our duty, and all will be well."

Final Remarks – Defense

Solomon then rose to address the jury. He began very humbly in his words, and put to the jury the complications in defending Mosse, stating he had never tried a criminal case of this nature in his career.

"Gentlemen of the jury, thus far in this case I feel that I have tried to do my duty. I feel that I have attempted to do simply what was right. I feel that I have attempted to do my duty towards

95

the court, towards the council, towards the jury, and particularly towards the defendant. I feel further that the responsibilities connected with this case have been too much and are too much for one of my experience. I feel that I have made a great many mistakes in the case. In rising to address you for the last time I feel that it would be impossible for me to properly present to you the defense in this case. I have so felt during the trial and appreciate now my inability to cope with the able council on the other side. They are men who in this class of cases have had great experience, and have no superiors in this county in the prosecution of criminal cases. They are men who are fresh from the fields of victory in this particular kind of prosecution."

This approach, no doubt an honest one, was carefully chosen by Solomon to show his humility in order to connect with the jury on a human level more so than as an authority figure. He continues, "I won't attempt to say anything for the purpose of pleasing the court or the purpose of pleasing the people in general. I have simply one object in view, one thing simply and that is to stand between this man and those who are trying to bring him to his grave: and I desire to do that fairly, honestly, without any sort of tricks, without any resort to sympathy, without any resort to any kind of chicanery."

Solomon made use of the next few minutes of his speech to show sympathy for Thiel's family. He expressed to the jury that both he and Mosse felt deep sorrow for what happened on that September day, and in defending Mosse it was not intended to bring any grief to the family; he said, "I appreciate the horrors of his death. I appreciate the sorrows of his family; that I could with them mingle tears over his grave."

Solomon then referred to the court as a temple of justice and said the jury should think of the courthouse as "a holy place, a place for serious consultation." Solomon went on to draw a connection to Pontius Pilate as the judge in the prosecution of Jesus Christ, and the manner in which public jeers and claims had been made against Mosse. He claimed, that just as Pilate was cajoled by the crowds chanting *crucify him! crucify him!* to send Jesus to the cross, the jury should not be persuaded by remarks made around Dixon to send Mosse to his death.

Solomon spent a great deal of time revisiting the severity of sending an innocent to condemnation; he said, "If you punish an innocent man you can never in this world, or in the world to come, recover from it, your conscience would be continually proding [*sic*] until you knew no peace, no rest, and right here let me state this proposition to you that you are not alone trying the question as to whether that boy is innocent or guilty."

He then spoke of Mosse's work ethic, and his view of his role in defending Mosse; he said, "I believe in communities where people start poor; where the youngest boy can start honestly with a desire to work and make a position in the world. Nobody believes that all the goodness, that all the virtue, that all that is great is contained in gilded palaces. I say that an honest man is the noblest work of God...I present him to you as a laboring man and I say that shall not be considered by you as evidence of guilt. I stand here speaking to you for the poor. I stand here pleading for the lonely. I stand here urging you to give that boy a trial just as thoroughly, just as honesty, just as fairly as you would the richest man in this courtroom."

Solomon also made mention that he felt as though he himself was on trial in the aspect of ridicule by the prosecution. Morrison had pointed out that Solomon was not poor, that he was "no pauper," and questioned the reasons behind Solomon taking on the case.

"I desire to say that I have earned my living always just as fully and honestly as the counsel on the other side and I have not drawn any salary from the county of Lee in doing so."

Solomon then re-counted the evidence, the series of events which took place in the days leading up to, and after Thiel's body was discovered. He dissected the evidence further, especially noting that when Mosse did return to the Spiller home the day of the murder, he had no blood on his clothes. He closed his speech with more words reflecting God and justice and the duty before the jury.

"There is no motive proved. You can't convict out of revenge, or malice. The deceased is gone; nothing can bring him back. Nothing you can do will right his injury. If you are influenced by that motive nothing but harm can come of it for it will only blind you to the actual evidence and to real justice. Revenge and malice actuate criminals, actuate the bad. They do not enter into the hearts of Christians or of justice. There is no place for them in God's universe, or in his plan of life. He has cast them out. They are but avenging spirits of the damned, of the wicked, of Satan himself. Let them not enter into this temple of justice…Here you will do as you would be done by. Here you will act as if one of your own was on trial. Others may laugh and jeer for upon them is not the responsibility. But you will do justice in mercy. Mercy is one of God's attributes, one that you will use in attempting to administer his laws."

Solomon then ended by reciting a tailored version of Portia's speech from William Shakespeare's *The Merchant of Venice*:

"The quality of mercy is not strain'd:
It droppeth as the gentle rain from heavens
Upon the place beneath: it is twice blesse'd:
It blesseth him that gives, and him that takes:
'Tis mightiest in the mightiest: it becomes
The throaned monarch better than his crown:
His scepter shows the force of temporal power
The tribute to awe and majesty,
Wherein doth sit the dread and fear of kings;
But mercy is above this sceptered sway;
It is enthroned in the hearts of kings,
It is an attribute to God himself,
And earthly power doth then show likest God's
Which mercy summons justice. Therefore,
Though justice be your plea, consider this –
That in the courts of justice none of us
Should see salvation: we do pray for mercy,
And that same prayer doth teach us all to render the deeds of mercy."

Morrison then began his closing address, harshly attacking Solomon, and for much of his closing, continued to ridicule Solomon, and only briefly spoke directly about Mosse. He also spoke to Solomon's assertion that he was inexperienced in such a case, arguing that Solomon had expertly performed his duty as a defense attorney.

"Will you come down with me now from realms of poetry and song, where Mr. Bethea so nicely landed you, to the facts of this case, as detailed to you by the witnesses…The gentleman took great pains to close by reciting from Shakespeare on the qualities and beauties of mercy. Probably, however, he does not admire that more than you or I. If you are fond of Shakespeare and want to read it I invite you, when this trial is over, to go to your homes and read it. It has nothing to do with this case; it is only produced to draw you away from the real issues of this case."

He went on to say Solomon was chock-full of "hifalutin [*sic*] talk," which was only intended to please the people in the courtroom and the jury, and on the subject of having to live with falsely sending an innocent man to a life of everlasting punishment, said, "My friend, Mr. Bethea, even at the marriage of *his* son or daughter may have the thought go rushing through *his* mind that he has assisted in turning the defendant loose on an unprotected and helpless community. It may come to him in his dreams, as he says, as he discourses eloquently."

Morrison also spoke to Solomon's notion that the horror of Thiel's murder need not be addressed in closing.

"...where is the place then, where may we go to discuss that; shall nothing be known as to how the crime was perpetuated? You, the jury, are compelled to fix the punishment, and how can you do so intelligently unless you know how atrocious the crime was."

He then brought up Solomon's decision to take the case without pay. He accused Solomon of at one time desiring a wage in defending Mosse. This was not substantiated, but Morrison continued, "Is it not true that when the people sent you down to Springfield to make laws, you drew a salary from the state? Did you not get five dollars a day from December until almost after harvest?"

He then accused Solomon to have wasted three hours of the jury's time by citing cases in which innocent men had been sent to prison and guilty men had gone free.

"I think I am safe in saying that he has not read a case that was tried since the invention of the steam engine...But those days have all passed away, we are glad to see them go. They have gone with witchcraft, gone with the whipping post, gone with slavery."

Solomon, in his closing speech, put it to the jury that it was a higher wrong to convict an innocent than it was to allow a guilty man to go free. Morrison gravely rebuked this theory, saying, "When, gentlemen, to follow Mr. Bethea's reasoning to its conclusion, would take us to anarchy; this government could not live, crime and murder would run riot, and our streets red with blood."

Morrison then relaxed his criticism of Solomon and turned to the case. He made direct assertions to the jury that the witness testimony was solid, no doubt linking Mosse to not only the area of the culvert where Thiel was found, but to Thiel himself. It was the testimony of children, specifically Louie Dixon, which initially marked Mosse.

"Now I want to tell you that the eyes of those little fellows, when their attention is called to anything, are brighter than ours; their impressions are stronger and more correct. They have not the cares of life, the cares of business that you and I have."

Morrison then spoke to Solomon's claims that witness testimony was unreliable in that he told the jury no man actually saw the crime committed, nor could several wholly identify Mosse. Criminals steal away to commit their crimes in secret, was Morrison's assertion, furthermore, he said, "The sun has not touched him; he is away from those influenced that tan can color the skin; he has been going through such a process as one does on a bed of sickness; he becomes a changed man; his acquaintances hardly recognize him, so great is that change. This is particularly so with dark persons. And yet, Mrs. Flatt, after all this, dared say he is not the man…"

In regard to Mosse being seen several times near the culvert, Morrison de-bunked the defense's claim that he was looking for work in the area, asking the jury, "Do men actually, looking for work, act thus? Do they not remain in town, and enquire of farmers as they come in? This man was, all at once, seized with a great desire to work, and in the immediate vicinity of the culvert, where poor Thiel lay in his impoverished grave."

Morrison brought up many good points as to validity of Mosses' testimony, citing his early remarks when arrested to be vague, rattled with "I don't know," and confusions about the chain, ring and spade. It was firmly put in the mind of the jury to question if Mosses' statements were true or false claims to try and cover his tracks early on, and Morrison did so just as eloquently as Solomon had purportedly sidetracked the jury with his *poetry and song*.

Morrison then spoke to Marshall Woodyatt's behavior in locating Mosse after the body was discovered; apparently Solomon has described Woodyatt's actions as that of a witch-hunt. He put to the jury that when Woodyatt set out to find the guilty man by walking the roads, stopping at homes along the way to trace the whereabouts of a man seen in the area the day of the murder, he was just in doing so.

"Should he be censured for it? Should he be characterized as a Sleuth hound? Had it been your child or mine sleeping beneath that culvert in death's cold embrace, placed there by the cruel hand of a butcher and a murderer, we would not feel that way."

Again, Morrison re-counted Mosse's behavior when he was apprehended, the question as to whether or not Mosse attempted to throw the watch chain away, and why would Woodyatt check his pockets anyway? Morrison re-stated the evidence of that day, saying again that Woodyatt found a ring in Mosse's pocket. It is still curious just how a ring found at the scene of the crime several days later, after hundreds of people had been through the area, became the one in question. Still, he said Solomon's theory that the ring had been placed at the scene to incriminate Mosse was false.

Morrison also spoke of the knife found at the scene, and the claim that Mosse lost his knife bailing hay at Hetler's place.

Morrison stated that had this been brought to light before trial, "I would have sent men, by the hundreds to search for it. He has sent no one. I would have searched every foot of ground, every spear of hay. I would have found that knife if it was still in existence. I would have said to every man I met, from the day of my arrest to this moment: Go in the name of justice; find that knife, I know it is there; it will break the chain; it will clear the dark clouds away; it will save my dear life; it will wash away the foul stain."

Morrison insisted that the motive, of which Solomon said there was none, was in-fact that Thiel had money. It was reported that the day before the murder Thiel had a considerable sum and that when he was discovered, his pockets were turned inside out and blood was stained inside the pocket lining.

"We cannot tell how much money he had; Thiel and his murderer alone knew, and Thiel's lips are sealed forever."

He continued by criticizing Mosse's alibi, which was hung on Maggie Smith's testimony that she was with Mosse that day. This criticism came because Maggie recalled being with Mosse until after three and he was not seen again until around six o'clock. He then attacked the testimony of Mrs. Barbra Spiller, in that she said she may tell a lie to protect Mosse.

"I am glad this community is not as bad as she. I am glad the world is better. If we were all like her and would swear to a falsehood to acquit a murderer this nation would perish, we would soon go back to the dark ages, human life and human blood would be cheap, and a reign of terror, such as this world never saw, would prevail."

He then closed by speaking to life's preciousness, and that Thiel, a bright, young ambitious man, would never be able to experience such joy, "Oh! how every thing that lives loves life." He said to the jury, "You will teach every man that comes before you that punishment follows crime as surely and unerringly as death follows life...you cannot bring back Frank Thiel. You cannot put life in that bleeding clay; but you can protect every other boy; you can protect society; by dealing with this man as the stern realities of this case demand. Gentlemen, I have done; this case rests with you. I thank you sincerely. Your honor, I have done."

Part 6: "Last Scene in the Tragedy!"

At half-past eight o'clock on the morning of January 27, 1886, Mosse took his seat in front of the jury. When Solomon came into the courtroom, Mosse stood up and politely extended his hand to Solomon. They shook hands and sat back down. It was painfully obvious that Mosse was not at ease. He kept lacing his fingers together on his lap, then un-lacing them and would twist his mustache. He shifted in his chair, crossing and re-crossing his legs. It was said, "...there was plainly unusual anxiety in his eyes and over his face was spread a deathlike pallor."

Mosse waited for the moment he would learn, "...whether he was to be strangled to death like a dog, imprisoned for the balance of his days on earth in the walls of a penitentiary or liberated." The representative for the jury rose to his feet and spoke.

"We the jury find the defendant guilty in the manner and form found as charged in the indictment and fix his punishment at imprisonment for his natural life in the State penitentiary."

Mosse did not move a muscle. There was not a sound in the courtroom, leaving the few people in attendance to believe him to be a man of iron nerve. Solomon leaned over and offered a few words of consolation and made a formal motion to have the case re-heard which was noted in the court records, and in due course denied.

"It's hard," was all Mosse said to Solomon, and was taken back to jail.

It was noted, on the first ballot cast by the jury that two votes were *not guilty*, ten were *guilty*, and six were for *hanging*. Neatly wrapped in a matter-of-fact sentence, the *Telegraph* ended the announcement as follows: "And thus ends one of the most exciting murder trials ever witnessed in this section of the state."

That night Mosse had a few visitors, one of which was a Frenchman who lived in south Dixon. The man was there to help Mosse write letters to friends, but was compelled to leave because Mosse was so unnerved he was, "crying like a child."

Passing Sentence – Judge Brown

On January 29, at around nine o'clock in the morning, Judge Brown then addressed Mosse directly to present the final sentence. He asked Mosse to stand up, and then told him to step closer so he would not miss a single word.

"After a fair and impartial trial, continuing through ten days, you have been convicted of the murder of Frank C. Thiel, and your punishment fixed at confinement in the penitentiary for your natural life."

Judge Brown himself re-counted the evidence provided in the case, the witness testimony and what was observed around town of Mosse's affiliation with Thiel. He firmly told Mosse that he believed all the information brought by the prosecution was accurate and there was not a doubt in his mind that Mosse was the guilty man.

"The crime of which you have been convicted was one of the most wanton and cruel crimes that was ever perpetuated within the State of Illinois….There is no question in my mind, but that on the day Thiel was murdered, you prevailed upon him to go with you into the country, under the assurance that he would sell an album to a Miss. Maggie Smith, and when you reached an unfrequented place, out of sight of dwelling houses, you deliberately and cruelly deprived him of life."

Additionally Brown told Mosse he was to spend five days each year in solitary confinement. He then went on to condemn Mosse as a monster, saying that for a sum of no more than 75 dollars, he took a young man's life. He even spoke of the cattle that first discovered the body.

"The circumstances attending the finding of the dead body of Thiel were most remarkable. Dumb beasts were terrified at your crime and became your accusers."

He then went on to tell Mosse he was lucky the jury spared his life, and that they showed mercy, where he did not in killing Thiel. His final statements made to Mosse were some of the most terrible, callous words spoken throughout the trial. Staring Mosse straight in the face, Judge Brown said the following:

"I have deliberately come to the conclusion that the only safe place for the willful murderer is the grave. If ever a man was worthy of death, you are the man: if a more cruel crime was ever committed it has not yet been revealed…I beseech you to indulge no hope of pardon…When the prison door closes behind you, it will not be opened to you until your body has come out for burial…Dressed in a felon's garb, you will be marched out to the labor assigned to you; day after day, week after week, month after month, year after year, until the last grain of sand shall run out of the dial of your life…The only solace a life convict can possibly have is the religion of Jesus Christ…I commend you to Him as the sinner's friend…"

Mosse stood there in front of Judge Brown, again not moving a muscle, not a word spilling from his lips. He was frozen in this moment; it was surprising his legs did not drop out from underneath his body. His eyes remained fixed on Judge Brown's eyes, his mouth aching to part and speak, but he simply could not, swallowed dry, and was led away to the Lee County Jail once again.

Final Interview

The *Telegraph* ventured a final interview with Mosse the evening before he was to be taken prison. The reporter noted that although it was difficult to interview him as a result of the language barrier, he felt a good show of Mosses' character came of the interview. Mosse was again described as a man of "low cunning," and that his conduct in the week following the murder was "remarkable for a man of ordinary intelligence."

The *Telegraph* first asked him if he had any siblings. Mosse said he had one brother, who died when Mosse was an infant and that he had a sister, but she died of tuberculosis at the age of 20, and again he said his mother died when he was one year old. After he spoke these words about his family, Mosse broke down completely, "weeping quite bitterly." After he regained composure, he said his father was still living but that he was too poor to, in any way, help his son, although he had sent him three letters while he was in jail.

Mosse went on to tell the reporter he had desired to speak to Judge Brown after his sentence was read, but he was afraid he would break down in the courtroom and he did not know how to say what he felt well enough in English to open his mouth.

When asked what he thought of the sentence, Mosse replied, "It was pretty hard on an innocent man."

Mosse also told the reporter that during his time in jail, Mr. and Mrs. Edwards and the deputies were all very kind to him but reports of him receiving cakes and flowers were not true. When asked whether or not he felt he could ever prove his innocence, Mosse said, "I don't think I can, but I am innocent all the same. I have not any idea who done it…I did not get a fair trial. Nobody but myself know it, but I am sure I did not."

In regard to the trial itself, Mosse said he did not feel the witnesses were accurate in their testimony.

"There was too much guessing," he said. Mosse was confident that Solomon did the very best job he could have, but that there, "was too much guessing by the witnesses…The witnesses did more guessing than anything else and it taint so at all. I had some witnesses on my side that said they would not tell the truth when they could tell the truth just so well as the other witnesses on the other side. The way they punish me I think they are use the witnesses on the other side and not use my witnesses at all. They did use my witnesses when they benefit the other side."

It is clear from his answers that Mosse, in fact spoke poor English and it was difficult for him to articulate just exactly what he intended to say. The *Telegraph* then took their leave as others, among them Maggie Smith and a Catholic priest, were waiting to speak with him.

Mosse and Smith were heard talking about who the *real* guilty man might have been, the *Telegraph* noting, "she taking it for granted that Mosse was innocent."

In the small hours of the morning of February 1, 1886, at 3:20 a.m., Sheriff Edwards took Mosse and three other prisoners to the train station and boarded the Central and headed south toward LaSalle. Observers watched as Mosse was put in iron handcuffs and chained to another prisoner, noting he looked not in the least bit happy. After a long evening in the jailhouse speaking with Maggie Smith, the girl he was to marry, the train whistle blew in the night and the heavy wheels began their slow turn on the rail. Joseph Mosse was headed for his forever-home in the penitentiary at Joliet.

One month shy of 26-years after Mosse was found guilty of murder, his life sentence was commuted on December 18, 1911, and he was released on Christmas Day. After spending a quarter of a century in the Joliet Penitentiary, the 47-year-old Joseph Mosse was free to go after saving a guard from a violent assault by another prisoner. Mosse was reported as saving at least two officers from certain death, if not life-threatening injuries, while he was retained in the Joliet facility.

Mosse had not a single blemish on his prison record and spent his nearly 26 years as a laborer making shoes, quietly serving his time. He was viewed by the guards as always being a genial and kind man, never complaining, virtually going unnoticed amid his fellow inmates.

The officer Mosse rescued in the assault made a public statement which was printed in the December 23rd edition of the *Telegraph*. The guard, who was respected as one of the top guards working at the penitentiary, had arrived in the shoe department at 9 o'clock a.m. to begin his rounds. When he entered the shop the door slammed violently behind him and was held in place by a heavy hanging weight. The officer attempted to open the door but an inmate by the name of Honeck was quickly on him and proceeded to slice at his neck with a sharp shoe knife. Honeck came at the guard in such a fanatical rage that he managed to slice two five-inch gashes in the neck area, one gash going clean to the bone, but avoiding the jugular vein.

The guard tried his best to grapple with Honeck, but as told to the Board of Pardons shortly after his release from the hospital, he had lost so much blood that he was beginning to lose consciousness. At this time, Mosse sprang from his work bench, ran across the shop, and intervened.

"...Mosse came to my rescue, seized Honeck, stayed him from further execution upon me and after a short, violent struggle with great danger to himself, wrested the knife from Honeck and with the assistance of others, now arrived, secured him."

The guard remarked that he was absolutely positive he would have been killed had it not been for Mosse. There were others working in the shop that day, but they remained frozen at their stations until Mosse decided to get involved.

"I beg to observe that while attacks such as this are very rare, men like Mosse are probably more so, and when a circumstance such as I have just recited describes him, a premium should be placed on his loyalty and manliness."

It is strange and ironic to think that an act uncannily similar to what cost Mosse his freedom, is exactly what guaranteed his release. How could a man reason to slit another man's throat, but also reason to save a man from the same terrible fate?

His brave acts of standing between guard and inmate are what ultimately gained him his freedom; however the pardon board made it firmly known that this was no gift.

In the December 25th edition of the *Decatur Review*, E.A. Snively, a member of the state pardon board, addressed the question as to there being any sentiment in giving inmates Christmas pardons. He remarked that a holiday pardon was not favored among Illinois officials and that it was mere coincidence that governors of the past granted commutations or pardons on Christmas Day. Mosse was the main focus of the article as he was making front-page news across the state, the brief article out of Springfield ended abruptly, stating:

"Liberty to Mosse not Gift."

"Soon after Mosse saved the life of the prison official at Joliet, our board met and we called Mosse in. We told him there that we appreciated his act but gave him to understand that he could not expect freedom on that account alone. We considered his case however, from all angles, and his commutation followed. His pardon, though, was not a Christmas gift."

JOSEPH MOSSE,
To Be Pardoned From Life Sentence
on Christmas Day.

Joseph Mosse

Photo: The *Telegraph* on Tuesday, December 19, 1911

Mosse never again appeared in the local papers, barring later accounts of the murder in the 1950's when a columnist decided to investigate the origins of the name Bloody Gulch Road. Where he went from Joliet is unknown, but one can imagine he wanted to get as far away from the state that took nearly 26 years of his young life and locked it behind bars.

Perhaps the culprits were the black-faced singing men outside of the General Store, or perhaps the murderer of another Gately and Co. salesman just weeks afterward, was the guilty man. Why this coincidence, briefly mentioned in the newspaper, was never investigated is unknown. Mosse was in jail at the time of this other murder, which, again, was said to be very similar to how Thiel was killed. Was someone stalking these Gately Bible Salesmen for their receipts? Was there some religious motivation to murder Bible salesmen? Was there a murderer who knew or stalked both victims?

Miss Maggie Smith may have driven a wedge between the men, causing the ill-fated death: a crime of true passion that turned a man of honor and distinction into a monster. Or simply, perhaps Mosse was in the wrong place at the wrong time, trying to earn an honest living wage by working at the farms near the crime scene. Perhaps his acquaintance with Thiel was what made him the marked man. Perhaps he became an easy target who spoke poor English and had not a single "friend" in town, as Solomon said in his opening remarks. He never admitted guilt, and still today it is up to all of us to discern whether or not Mosse, *beyond a reasonable doubt,* murdered the young traveling Bible salesman from Elgin.

Solomon Bethea, having passed away in 1909, did not experience the satisfaction of seeing the man he firmly believed innocent in 1886 receive a pardon. While he stood up in court, and in the ensuing years, Solomon held steadfast to his confidence in Mosse's innocence. If the pardon had been granted two years earlier, it would have surely brought an immense sense of justice and some measure of happiness to Solomon's later years, which he spent alone, and according to surviving distant relatives, full of sadness after Katherine's death and the passing of his mother and father.

Chapter 4

Kinfolk: South Carolina to Lee County
The Bethea Family

William Wilson Bethea
History of Lee County, Chicago: H.H. Hill and Co. 1881

Solomon Hicks Bethea was born on May 20, 1852 to William Wilson Bethea and Emily Green (Ferguson) Bethea. Solomon's father was an incredibly strong-willed man of good repute, and raised his boy to be the same.

William Wilson Bethea

William Wilson Bethea was born on May 15, 1812 in Marion County, South Carolina, where many of the Bethea family settled after emigrating from England around 1700. The first Bethea to arrive on America's shore was "English" John Bethea, who crossed the Atlantic Ocean from Great Britain to Norfolk, Virginia.

He then moved to Nansemond County, and with the "Widow Lady Upton," had two sons, John and Tristram. John Jr. had two sons, William and John III. "Sweatswamp" William (third generation) had four sons, John IIII, Goodman, Philip and Jesse. Goodman Bethea (fourth generation) had two sons, Philip and Jesse. Philip (fifth generation) had at least four sons, Goodman, Philip, John Washington and William Wilson (sixth generation), making Solomon a seventh generation descendant from "English" John Bethea (Bethea, et.al.).

William Wilson moved with his family to Mitchell, Indiana; from there they relocated to northern Illinois in 1835 after the death of his father, Philip. His mother, Mary Millsap, came to Dixon with her four boys. William's three brothers did not stay long in Dixon, and all moved to other parts of the country.

William laid claim to land in Palmyra Township in the spring of 1835 at the age of 23. William remarked that he was first attracted to Dixon when he heard John Dixon was the only man "with any money" who would gladly give work to any man who asked. William's first dollar was earned by working for John Dixon, and he forever would make Lee County his home.

William's young adult life could be argued as one of pure tragedy. At the age of 21 he married a Miss. Irena Fender, a beautiful young woman of 18 from Maryland, on December 19, 1833 in Mitchell, Indiana. Nearly nine months to the day later, Irena gave birth to a baby girl, Sally, on September 25, 1834. For 10 months the family was happy; William out cultivating his land, Irena in the home tending their baby girl. The joy of a young family all came to a halt on November 16, 1836, when Sally died. The terrible shock of losing a child would soon be over-shadowed when Irena gave birth to a second daughter, Polly, one month after Sally's funeral on December 20, 1836. Polly lived to be one year old and died on January 25, 1837. The Bethea home would be silent for a year and a half—no babies crying, no birthday celebrations—only mournful visits to the Palmyra cemetery, one in the Fall when leaves begin to a turn brilliant red and orange, and one caught forever in the coldest depths of Winter.

Despite these tragedies, Irena became pregnant again. The Bethea's would try once more for the joyful family; for the children to help tend the farm, to perhaps bring home ducklings from Sunday school on Easter. William would try again with dreams of trips in the wagon to town for supplies and Christmas mornings spent lounging in his union suit, laughing children on his knee. But no matter how sincere or heartfelt his wishes and dreams, William was doomed to misfortune.

On the morning of July 10, 1838, William's young wife died at the age of 22 giving birth to his first son, John W. Bethea, named for his brother. It was not uncommon for women to die in childbirth. Complications were a worrisome reality.

An educated guess leads one to believe the family suffered from some common illness such as cholera or pneumonia, both having the capability to result in death quickly after taken ill. A common phrase of the time was probably spoken around town of William's losses, *"They had sickness in the home."*

A widower with an infant son at the age of 26, William began teaching in an unfinished small frame school house nearby in Sugar Grove, Illinois, in addition to farming his modest homestead. In two-months' time, William would find himself completely alone when John died at the age of one month, 25 days.

A deep sadness overtook William, and in the years to come he would busy himself with hard work on the farm in addition to participating in community initiatives, one being to support whole-heartedly the railroad built in Lee County as he wished to secure a strong economy for the Dixon area. William along with Levi Gaston were designated the first Justices of the Peace in Dixon, at which time *Esq.* was added to his moniker. William was also elected Lee County Treasurer, holding the office for many years.

His 1863 candidacy announcement in the *Amboy Times* read as follows: "Should my desires meet your approbation and I succeed in the convention, and likewise at the polls in November, I will endeavor to discharge the duties of said office to the best of my ability. Should I not succeed, I will cordially give my support to the candidate receiving the nomination at the said Union Convention, as my motto is, *the Union now, henceforth and forever.*"

In the coming years William worked hard and bought up as much land as he could afford in the Palmyra area. The cost per acre during this time was approximately $2.08. In 1843 he purchased 320 acres, turning his small farmstead into a vast stretch of rolling land. His brother John Washington, and wife Margaret Jane Stewart, would also come to Lee County and purchase land. Margaret purchased a 40 acre tract four months after William's initial acquisition. John Washington would purchase an additional 80 acres in 1848-49, making the Bethea homestead a truly expansive farming operation. John and Margaret made investment in the Palmyra farm, never actually taking permanent residence with William, and moved to Rose Hill, Iowa in 1847.

On the farm William specialized in raising prize-winning horses. As listed in the Amboy Journal in 1873, the horses were described as "Monmouth Horses—All Work." William took home prizes for six of his horses that year at the Dixon Fair. William would build his estate to be quite breathtaking as seen in the sketch of his home in the *Lee County Plat Book* for 1872. There are even a few horses being corralled beside the home in this image, probably the likeness of the desirable Monmouth horses he bred.

RES. OF W.W. BETHEA.
SEC. 20 PALMYRA TP, LEE CO. ILL.

William Wilson Bethea residence Palmyra

Lee County Plat Book 1872

It took 12 painful years for William to recover from the loss of his entire family, and he would at last marry again to Emily Green Ferguson in 1850. Some might say the ordeal soured William, but he gave marriage and family-rearing another chance in 1852 when Solomon came along. William no doubt doted on the boy, but one wonders if he ever had moments of deep sorrow, perhaps catching a glimpse of his other little ones in Solomon's infant face.

As the years passed and Solomon grew into a strong little four-year-old, William and Emily decided to have another baby. At the age of 43, William became a father once again to another little boy. Solomon was to be a big brother, and in July of 1855 Emily gave birth to William Jr. Perhaps William was somewhat fated as a father, as this infant son died on March 21, 1856 at the age of 8 months, 3 days.

The photo following this text, taken of William late in life, clearly shows the toll life had taken. A man said to be, "of strong characteristics, public spirited, hospitable, energetic and devoted to truth," had years of loss etched into his honest face (Jennings).

William Wilson Bethea
Photo Courtesy of Loveland Museum

As William aged he enjoyed serving on the executive committee representing Palmyra for The Old Settler Days. The Old Settlers' Reunions were held in Dixon each summer. In June of 1874, Father Dixon was present and took his spot on the grandstand to hear the old hymns, old-time jokes and witty comic routines. 2,000 people were said to be in attendance and, "Nachusa among friends." "Nachusa" was Father Dixon's nickname as given by the Native Americans of the area, meaning "White Hair." The *Amboy Journal* kept with the Native American theme, and printed, "The Old Pioneers Hold a Pow Wow."

At the Old Settlers celebration of 1876, William, now 64 years old, was among the original pioneers to be called to the stage to, "come up and show off their good looks." The *Amboy Journal* remarked, "they were as fine looking company of elderly persons as one will ever see." This remark no-doubt raised a chuckle from the old folks reading the paper a few days later.

The main attraction at the reunions was the food. All the families set up picnic spots, parading a lavish spread of home-cookery, as many as the eye could see, and all shared their dishes. The wives of the old settlers were said to be *the best of cooks*, while the husbands, *the best of eaters*. One pioneer, Abijah Powers, known as the "Cattle King of Palmyra" shared the best beef around with those quick enough to get in line. Spirits were high, as many partook in Whitney's home-made wine made from his famous Siberian apples, and bellies were full, when a very special visitor took the stage.

A famous guest, not only by reputation in 1876, but by today's standards as well; known then as the "Plow King of Moline," John Deere, 72 years old, was in attendance and was first to take the stage.

"Gentleman—I am right glad to see you!, and hope old acquaintances will never be forgot."

The historic day would be marked once again when Dr. Everett introduced Colonel John Dement by way of saying, "It is not necessary to introduce a man whom everybody knows." Colonel Dement, blushing from being called from the crowd, was about to sit back down when Dr. Everett commanded, "Don't go away!"

Dr. Everett produced a cane, which was not just *any* cane, and began to address the crowd:

> "I have the honor on behalf of the people of Dixon of presenting you this cane. Presenting a cane, everybody knows, involves the necessity of making a speech […] This cane has some historic interest. It was made from the old walnut canoe which once belonged to the famous Indian warrior Black Hawk, and as you were amongst the afterwards distinguished men who were here in 1832, away out in the Indian country, far from civilization or any white settlement, when the militia of the state, together with a considerable force from the United States army, were called out to put down that famous Capt. Jack of the Prairie State, and as a large part of your life has been spent here among us, the people deem it peculiarly fitting at this time to present you this small testimonial of their esteem and good wishes."

Col. John Dement cane made from Black Hawk's walnut canoe

Loveland Community Museum Collection

Gold handle inscribed to Col. John Dement
Loveland Community Museum Collection

The pioneer picnics continued for a few more years until numbers dwindled to merely a few. One of the last mentions in the paper on May 5, 1886, listed only 20 or so settlers; then on September 4, 1889 the *Amboy Journal* noted another Old Settler's Picnic, at which Solomon Bethea delivered the address. During these years, the celebrations declined and times were fast changing from what William knew of his youth.

Emily passed away at the age of 61 on June 3, 1883. Her death certificate reports the cause of death to be gastritis following mucus. Gastritis is simply an erosion or irritation of the stomach lining (probably what we would call an ulcer and quite treatable today). She had been sick for six to eight weeks before her death. The *Amboy News* said of her, "She was among the earliest settlers of Lee County, and an estimable lady, having a large circle of acquaintances."

Emily Green Bethea Death Certificate
Courtesy of the Lee County Clerk, Nancy Nelson

William would live into his 80's, another ten years after Emily's death. Two-times a widower—but all the hardship William had suffered was not been in vain, as his only surviving child would grow to be a very remarkable man in family, community, politics and in his career. William had kept Solomon close to his heart at all times, though never limiting the young boy or shielding him from life's experiences. He raised Solomon to know the value of hard work and respect. He taught him to always work toward the greater good, to be active in the community and hold family above all else.

Hon. Solomon Hicks Bethea Ancestry*

"English" John Bethea— 1674-1735
    M: "Widow Lady" Upton— 1663-1685

"Virginia" John Bethea Jr.— 1705-1799
    M: Sarah Darby Bishop— 1704-xxxx

William "Sweat Swamp" Bethea— 1726-1784
    M: Sarah Goodman— 1730-1776

Goodman Bethea— 1759-1798
    M: Mary Council— 1756-xxxx

Philip Bethea— 1780-1834
    M: Mary Milsap— xxxx-xxxx

William Wilson Bethea— 1812-1893
    M: Emily Green Ferguson— 1820-1883

Solomon Hicks Bethea— 1852-1909
    M: Katherine Campbell Shaw— 1855-1893

  *   Birth/Death/Marriage records are incomplete
      Bethea ancestral dates shown are approximate.

Chapter 5

Solomon Hicks Bethea:
From the Farm to Federal Judge.

"Let judges also remember that Solomon's throne was supported by lions on both sides, let them be lions, but yet lions under the throne."

~ Francis Bacon

The name Solomon itself has come to represent, or in various translations mean "peace," or be an indication of "wisdom." Surely the most widely known *Solomon* in history was King Solomon, son of David. The name itself has its roots in Hebrew, and has long been associated with King Solomon, tying in closely with his position as a judge.

Sharing this name, it is of interest to note that both the biblical King Solomon and Solomon Hicks Bethea had something in common: the law. In the Book of Kings, there is a story of the Lord appearing to King Solomon in a dream, asking him what he would like, as in character traits or abilities. King Solomon's reply was, "Give therefore thy servant an understanding heart to judge thy people, that I may discern between good and bad…" The Lord granted King Solomon's request, impressed that he did not ask for riches, long life, or for any harm to come to his enemies, saying, "I have given thee a wise and an understanding heart; so that there was none like thee before thee, neither after thee shall any arise like unto thee."

One of the most well-known stories of judgment in the Bible is of King Solomon's, in which an infant was at stake. The story (Kings 3: 16-28), involved two *harlots* disputing the maternity of a child. They both lived in the same house, and birthed their babies a few days apart. One woman rolled onto her baby in her sleep, smothering it. The other woman charged that the children were switched in the night by the mother of the dead infant.

Solomon, in an incredibly unorthodox maneuver, suggested cutting the child in half, so both mothers could 'have the baby.' This 'judgment,' however gruesome, was ultimately a wise tactic of truth-seeking, as the real mother shrieked, "Let her have the child!" Solomon knew from her reaction that she was the real mother, and ruled in her favor to keep the baby.

This may simply be romancing a text, but none the less, this quality was also seen later in the way Solomon Bethea approached law and justice [he did not however stray to the wayside like the Biblical king, who *loved many strange women*, and angered the Lord]. As mentioned by many who knew him, Solomon's approach to law was virtually Puritanical in that his moral judgments, and whether or not he took a case seemed to rely heavily on his firm set of ethics, and on sympathy for the common man (as seen in the *Bloody Gulch Murder* case).

Solomon Hicks Bethea

Photo Courtesy of Loveland Museum

Solomon Hicks Bethea: The Beginning

Growing up on the farm, Solomon enjoyed the rural lifestyle as many boys did in those days, playing stick ball in the fields and helping his father. He rode horses nearly constantly, something that would become his passion and that he would later enjoy with his wife, Katherine Shaw. He first attended the district school, but according to his biography, as recorded by L.H. Jennings for the University of Michigan alumnus collection, he didn't spend long in the rural public school system:

"An incident while there illustrates the sturdiness of his character. One day the teacher sneeringly remarked upon the color of his hair: he took his books and left school, and completed his preparatory course for college at the Dixon Seminary, going back and forth six miles daily on his horse." Clearly, he was incredibly independent even as a youth.

Solomon was exceedingly successful in school and enrolled at the University of Michigan in 1868 at the age of 16. Always having a passion for the written word, he joined the Literary Department and was a member of the Adelphi Literary Society. A marked example of this was recorded in The *Telegraph* in 1884 when Solomon addressed the Palmyra Literary and Debating Society at the Town Hall, and gave an address entitled, "What to read, and how to read it." He was regarded as an industrious student, again having learned his work ethic from his father. He was a quiet young man but quickly gained the respect of his fellow students and teachers. He graduated Michigan on June 23, 1872, and returned to Dixon.

When he returned, William encouraged Solomon to make full use of his education. Solomon took his father's advice and his fervor for law and community involvement led him to the door of the law office of Eustace, Barge & Dixon, where he began to learn what was to be his life vocation and what would one day deliver him to the rank of Federal Judge. Solomon passed the bar in 1875 at the age of 22, and quickly established himself as a fine lawyer, commencing business on his "own hook," returning to practice with Judge Eustace. Solomon would also establish himself as a strong political figure in Dixon as a member of the Republican Party.

Solomon inherited both of his father's most desirable characteristics: his eye and mind for northern enterprise and his southern hospitality. "Solomon had almost a Puritan sense of right and wrong and the warmth of feeling and hospitality for friends." His ability as a lawyer was soon demonstrated, as well as his gift for the spoken word: "He possessed a good voice and stood high as an orator, not only in the court-room where he argued many cases important to the people of Illinois, but in the political arena was also known as a powerful speaker." (Jennings).

From his humble beginnings as a small-town lawyer, Solomon was destined for greater political accomplishments. His warm attitude toward fellow politicians and community quickly established Solomon as not only a talented politician and lawyer, but also as a "man of men." He would soon rise through the ranks in the political arena and become a renowned judge, as well as an 'unofficial' advisor and friend to many high-profile politicians, including President Theodore "Teddy" Roosevelt.

Law office of Solomon Hicks Bethea, date unknown. Solomon is 6th from the left, seated. Note his extensive law library, as well as the Black-crowned Night Heron taxidermy specimen, upper right-hand shelf, which may have been a gift from President Roosevelt.

Photo courtesy of the Lee County Historical Society

Solomon's Work in Dixon

Solomon acted as attorney in many Lee County cases, and his partnerships varied throughout his legal career. After graduating from the University of Michigan in 1872, Solomon studied law with the firm of Eustace, Barge and Dixon, a group of prominent lawyers known throughout northern Illinois, and he was admitted to the bar on May 12, 1876. Later, in addition to practicing solo for five years, Solomon partnered with John V. Eustace, Sherwood Dixon, his son, Henry S. Dixon, and C.B. Morrison.

In regard to politics, nothing much changes over time, as the war between Democrats and Republicans forever wages. In *Mertz's People's Union Mission Magazine*, published in 1905, this distinction was made all-too-clear, and Solomon took a sort of printed-beating via strong scrutiny of his Republican ties. An excerpt follows:

"Dixon is noted for quite a number of innovations and wonders. Dixson [*sic*], Ill. Is noted for her Chautauquas, for her great milk condensing factory and for not having a criminal conviction for over six years through the agency of prosecution.

"Dixon and Lee County are noted for political rings. At present the republican political machine is composed of the following politicians: M.J. McGowan, John Hughes, C.B. Morrison, S.H. Bathea [*sic*]. These are considered the "Big Four." They are in constant communication with the higher lights and stars of the republican party, they keep subordinate and local politicians posted and instructed, they are a sort of political encyclopedia for Lee county and their respective judicial and congressional districts."

The article went on to list every politician in the Lee County townships who were *in the pocket* of the "Big Four." This was mere political rhetoric of the times, but it is interesting to read none-the-less.

Solomon would also be elected Mayor of Dixon twice, serving in 1888 and 1889. Upon his arrival to Dixon from Chicago, the *Telegraph* reported Solomon, as mayor-elect, was met at the depot by a crowd, "...and with much parade and a brass band escorted to the city council rooms where he was duly inaugurated in the office to which he was elected on Monday."

As mayor, Solomon had to endure "The Water Works Problem." The Dixon Water Company had apparently done a substandard job of building Dixon's water supply system. According to reports in the *Telegraph*, the pipes were placed too near the surface, not deep enough to escape frost, in-turn virtually halting all of Dixon's water supply. And when it was not ice, the water pressure was also under scrutiny.

Somewhat comical, the paper reported on March 29, 1888, "That is not a spontaneous self flowing artesian well that causes the water to burst up on Galena street in front of the post office...A small water pipe leading from the main to a saloon bursted with disgust at the small amount of water used through it."

The *Telegraph* consistently reported in editorials that Solomon and the city council were acting fair and just in their decision to stop paying The Dixon Water Company until they would remedy the serious problem. The council and the company went back and forth, the company demanding back-payment for services and threatening to shut down the water all together—the council (and The Circuit Court) refusing both demands. The City of Dixon was crying out for artesian wells to be built (at the cost of about $8,000), and Solomon even took a trip to Chicago to examine their artesian well system. His diligence in tackling the issue was probably one of the reasons that Dixon's residents were sad to see Solomon leave his post as mayor.

As an attorney, the most famous of the cases Solomon tried was of course, the "Bloody Gulch Murder" trial. On the other end of the spectrum was an account of perhaps his most humorous case as reported in the *Amboy News* in 1885, only this time it was not about cattle first discovering a gruesome murder, but about a poor cow who lost her life, "by having her head caught in a salt barrel and becoming entangled in a wire fence."

A farmer, Thomas Drew brought suit for damages against W.D. Parker for, "carelessly leaving the salt barrel aforesaid upon the prairie, about which was coiled wire, by which the plaintiff's cow was caught in a trap and lost her life." Solomon was successful in arguing for Drew, as he secured an award of thirty-five dollars, with which it is assumed, Mr. Drew purchased a new cow. The article mentioned that "many fine points in law were discussed." For instance, if Mr. Parker had left the empty salt barrel on his own land, as his attorney, D. D. O'Brien, tried to argue, the cow would have been trespassing.

The humorous cases do not end there, however. In April of 1886 a case, known as "Geese in Court" would make the front page of the *Telegraph*. Goose Hollow, a then "suburb" of Dixon, located in Ogle County, was the "scene of the terrible outrage," in which three geese were reported as stolen and then sold at the Waverly House (a boarding house) in Dixon.

The culprit was Thomas Moran, a poor man who could afford no council. Much in the same way Joseph Mosse would secure the council of Solomon; A.K. Trusdell volunteered to act as chief council. He then appointed Solomon and attorney Mr. Crabtree to "hold a consultation with the prisoner," in hopes of figuring out just what happened the day the geese went missing and ended up on dinner plates at the Waverly House.

With the geese in the bellies of "greedy traveling men," it was apparent that Robert Steadman's "goose was cooked," the Goose Hollow man who claimed to have owned the geese (The *Telegraph*). Council, it was reported, planned to enter a plea of insanity on behalf of Moran, but the *Telegraph* clearly disagreed with this notion: "Thus it will appear that the ulprit [*sic*] is really a genius—having a talent for making money quite equal to a stock market broker or a railroad magnate."

The story as it appeared in the paper was published as an idiosyncratic way to sell more papers, as the last line was, "Now is your time to subscribe for the *Telegraph*." And who could blame them? The high hopes of such a goofy story was quickly snuffed out when the court proceedings proved to be anything but interesting.

"The members of the bar, individually and collectively, appeared to be uncommonly dull and we might say stupid," the *Telegraph* reported three days later when the trial began. Solomon probably took no notice of this remark as he understood it was a sort of media circus the readers of newspaper were after, not run-of-the-mill legal "mumbo gumbo." In fact, the case was so boring; *Telegraph* reporters left the court room before any verdict was announced. Perhaps Moran's goose was cooked as well, that is unless his insanity plea went through.

In addition to serving two terms as mayor of Dixon, Solomon also served as master in chancery of the Circuit Court of Lee County for ten years. He was made United States Attorney for the Northern District of Illinois in 1898, "a position which he filled with signal fidelity and ability," according to his biography in *The Report of the American Bar Association*, and which would eventually lead to his appointment as Federal Judge for the Northern District of Illinois by President Theodore Roosevelt in 1905.

Solomon's Sense of Humor

Though Solomon took his work as lawyer, prosecutor and judge very seriously, he was certainly not without a sense of humor. In 1885, the lawyers and doctors of Dixon came together to form a baseball team, the "Never Sweats." They played against the "Rippers," a team made up of local merchants. Game day, June 19th, produced, "A large crowd of people in carriages…and the contest was much enjoyed by all."

The article chronicling the game read as though Mark Twain had written it—full of satire, and a certain cheerfulness. "While some of the Doctors and Lawyers dodged the balls instead of making any attempt to catch them there were some right sharp players in the game." Also poking fun at the players, the *Telegraph* reported that, "It is requested that parents chain up their small boys tomorrow morning so that they may not be crushed by the falling players."

The focal point of the article, however, was the question of who would act as umpire for the game, as it was certainly the most dangerous position, due to the complete lack of experience by all of the players taking the field:

"There seems to be considerable trouble in finding a man bold enough to act as umpire. Wildly pitched balls and flying bats slipping from delicate hands will cause many sore shins and bloody noses, without doubt…An experienced ball player says that he would act as umpire if a long box with a peek-hole for observation from the top could be furnished for him to stand in." After much debate as to who would be brave enough to man home base, none other than Solomon Hicks Bethea agreed to put himself in such peril.

The game was won by the "Never Sweats" in a close match, beating the "Rippers" by one point, for a final score of 21-20. As if umpiring wasn't embarrassment enough for Solomon, he agreed the next year to act as team mascot for the "Never Sweats." One can only imagine what sort of get-up the team persuaded their attorney talisman to wear, but no doubt he fulfilled the task with much enthusiasm.

Another instance of Solomon's humorous side was demonstrated when he returned from a business trip to Chicago, bringing with him a copy of the book, "Peck's Bad Boy" as a gift for his father. The book contains stories akin to those of *Dennis the Menace*, in which a boy torments his poor father in the most comical ways one can imagine. Perhaps this was a small peek into Solomon's behavior as a child, when he may have been a bit of a trickster—and, when paired with Jennings' account of Solomon being removed from the country school, it seems as though he had an aptitude for mischief. When examining his adult life, it was often his humorous side, cleverness, and his inherent *zeal*, that brought minor troubles his way.

The Chicago Years

Solomon began his career in "big politics" in 1882 when he became a member of the Illinois State Legislature, but well before election to state office he had already begun the task of addressing National issues. His attention to the political climate after the Civil War would be a stepping stone in his acquisition of party stature. Solomon identified himself as an Independent Republican, and delivered a speech at the Garfield Club in Chicago in 1880, endorsing the Republican Party as leading the country in a new direction after the war, saying: "Forget the war if you can but insist upon all of its legal results" (The *Amboy Journal*). Although Solomon was only nine-years-old when the war broke out and 13 when it came to a close, there is little doubt he often over-heard his father speaking about what was happening in the southern states.

In endorsing James A. Garfield for President of the United States, Solomon established his ties to the Republican Party, and henceforth would always be active in the highest ranks of United States politics. In this same address, Solomon made reference to an array of issues affecting the United States in 1880, his argument being that the Democratic Party was largely inconsistent throughout the war and in the years which followed; "...Republicans are right and the Democrats are wrong" (the *Telegraph*).

He also addressed the financial climate of the times: "They [Democrats] have been against green-backs when the nation's life demanded them, and for them when our prosperity demanded coin; and to-day if they got complete control, the visionary element of their party, I verily believe, would bring us to ruin..." (*The Telegraph*).

In his address endorsing Garfield, Solomon said,

"The Democrats say there shall be no sumptuary laws. That means that they are in favor of wiping out all laws restraining the sale of intoxicating drinks; all laws in our state known as dram shop laws. The American people are not ready to accept such a doctrine and never will be. The temperate, law abiding citizen everywhere will insist upon the restraint of the sale of liquor."

Solomon, who was never a drinking man, although early relatives very much took to the bottle, was against alcohol in every way. It was recorded of the original Bethea clan in *A History of Marion County*, that, "They all loved liquor and, except old Philip, drank it to excess, till after middle life, when they tapered off, and by the time of old age became perfectly abstemious, and this was especially the case with William, James and Parker." These men would have been cousins to Solomon's grandfather Philip, and there is no record of Solomon's side of the Bethea family to have ever had issues with alcohol.

This is marked in a letter written by Solomon's Aunt Margaret Jane Stewart Bethea to her granddaughter in October of 1905. [Note: her misspelling of words has been preserved as it shows her level of education, as well as demonstrates the manner in which she spoke]. She wrote of a visit to Chicago, Illinois:

"I am afraid they don't live very good, a good many of them, so much drinking and swaring in these cities and all kinds of wickedness going on. Solie is a very sober man. I was afraid that he drank being such a prominent man, but noe he don't tuch it. He said he made some enemies at first because he wouldent drink. He brought the subject up soon pretty soon after I met him on drinks. I expect he thought that as he was a lawyer I would think mabe he drank. He seemed ancious to let me now that he dident. He seemed so glad to see me. He nows I am opposed to such things."

There is another trait that speaks to Solomon's character. Amid political scandal and political life versus personal life, something which is still seen in spades today, Solomon truly lived the life he portrayed politically and only once was his political integrity questioned when he ran for the Legislature in 1882. "Will 'Sol' be led by the 'machine politician' to support Cullom? [Shelby M. Cullom, 17th Illinois Governor, 1877-1883] We shall see whether he proposes to be a tool or a man" (*The Dixon Sun*).

It was obvious from his early political involvements that Solomon would be active in the Republican Party, and go on to run for a seat in the State Legislature. In June of 1882, Solomon announced his candidacy, subject to the action of the County Commission. The reception of this news by Lee County was very positive, *The Amboy Journal* reporting:

"Mr. Bethea is a young man of ability, and a lawyer of rapidly rising fame. We are glad to know that his prospects of receiving the nomination are particularly good. If he receives it, his election is, of course, assured, and we are glad to feel that our County is likely to be represented in the next Legislature by a man who will so well represent us."

Solomon secured the republican ticket again in February of 1883, and it was quickly established that he was no cog in the political machine. News of his election was reported in the *Dixon Sun*: "[Solomon] is a republican of short standing, but, long enough it seems, to convince him of the corruption of party management and of the usual rascality practiced within the party to secure nominations and offices."

Immediately after his election, Solomon introduced a bill to regulate primaries and caucuses. He insisted that it should become law because office-selecting institutions were corruptly managed. Although Solomon was "selected and nominated by a clique to vote for Cullom," his political motives remained with what he thought best for the state of Illinois. The *Dixon Sun* went on to report, "But it [the bill] speaks well for his personal honesty if secretly he despises the methods by which he was advanced. The bill he has introduced, in its purpose is evidence of this."

Despite his success and warm-welcome in the State Legislature, Solomon returned to Dixon in 1884 to continue his private practice, and married Katherine Shaw. One reason Solomon may have ducked out of Springfield, although accounts in local papers often referred to him as having done a fine job and that the people would love to have him as their Representative again, was probably connected to Katherine's frequent fluctuations in health. Although she did not pass away until 1893, she had several bouts of decline due to her tuberculosis. These were marked when newspapers reported Solomon as having relocated to Colorado in 1885, though he would return again a year later and resume his law practice in Dixon.

It was in 1885 that the *Amboy Journal*, in an editorial, again called for Solomon to once more run for office stating, "[Solomon] has already served in the State Legislature and did so with great credit to himself and reflected honor upon those who sent him. He is a gentleman of sterling worth and will represent this senatorial district in a manner satisfactory to the entire constituency."

Despite leaving the legislature, Solomon remained heavily involved in politics at the state-level. He was often chosen as a delegate to the Illinois State Republican Conventions, having served also once as the following: alternate, chairman, and as a Vice President of the Republican League, for the known years, 1880, 1886, 1887, 1888, 1890, 1896 and 1900. [Most likely he attended all conventions, barring the year 1885, but may have not been a delegate.]

In 1896, when the representatives of the State of Illinois held the convention to select who they would endorse for the Presidential nomination, Solomon made an appearance in the *New York Times*, as being none other than the instigator in what turned into a *hysterical* convention. Under the head line, "Illinois for McKinley. Great Victory for the Ohio Candidate in the State Convention," was written the general outline of what happened—how McKinley won:

"It is true that the form in which the resolution was adopted—the substitution of McKinley's name in the Cullom resolution—was due to the overzeal [*sic*] of a delegate who anticipated the regular McKinley indorsement [*sic*] which was to have been presented by the spokesman of his following…" The overzealous delegate turned out to be Solomon Hicks Bethea.

While it was thought and anticipated that Illinois' choice would be Shelby Moore Cullom, Senator Fuller of Belvidere mounted a chair, submitting a resolution for that to be the case, but after the cheering for Cullom subsided, the room filled with, "a cyclone of nays, hisses and groans." Clearly, the session was not over, and the Chairman declared he would keep the convention in session all night long [which, in the end, lasted a full 10 hours], or until they had reached a decision and both sides were heard.

This caused Senator Fuller to literally push his way through the crowd, take the platform in front of the 1,335 men in attendance, and deliver a speech in support of Cullom. There is no better way to describe what happened next, than to quote the *New York Times* directly:

"He barely had turned his back when Delegate S. H. Bethea of Dixon, anticipating Speaker Calhoun, jumped upon a chair and moved to substitute the name of McKinley for that of Cullom in the resolution. The demonstration that greeted the mention of McKinley was terrific. Two-thirds of the convention, and the thousands in the gallery, rose en mass and cheered for at least three-minutes, and the tempest was repeated when the Chair repeated the amendment."

And the rest, as they say, is history. The Ohioan would go on to the National Republican Convention, which took place in St. Louis, Missouri, less than one month after a devastating tornado had torn through the city, killing 280 people. He would also win the Presidency, and be sworn into office on March 4, 1897.

This anecdote runs deep in the telling of Solomon's character, however. Though it may have read as Solomon being unfriendly toward Cullom, quite the opposite was true. In his memoirs, *Fifty Years of Public Service*, Shelby Cullom wrote of his high regard for Solomon, even nodding at Bethea's *overzealous* demonstration during the 1896 convention. His recollections of Solomon are quoted directly:

"Humphrey [Judge J. Otis Humphrey, United States District Judge for the Southern District of Illinois] and Bethea I have always regarded as my two judges, as they were both appointed on my recommendation. Bethea was a man of very strong and positive character. These traits were so conspicuous that his manners were, by some, regarded as extremely dictatorial. He was highly educated, a student all his life, and a very cultivated man. At the same time he was a first-rate politician. I do not know of two more useful men to lead a floor fight in a convention than Bethea and Humphrey.

"Judge Bethea was my friend and supporter from the time I was elected to the United States Senate, in 1883, until his death. He made a splendid record as United States Attorney, and I am informed that during his incumbency of that office, he never lost a case before a jury. Very unfortunately, just when he reached the goal of his highest ambition, a Federal judgeship, his health failed. I have never for a moment doubted that had he lived and retained his health he would have made an enviable record on the bench."

Solomon's reputation continued to grow as an honest man of law, and on December 20, 1898, he was appointed United States District Attorney for the Northern District of Illinois by President McKinley. Solomon was active during the McKinley administration not only as a United States District Attorney, but he also acted as floor leader for the Republican convention of 1900. As recorded by Charles G. Dawes [U.S. Comptroller of the Currency 1898-1901, and 30th Vice President of the United States] in the book, *A Journal of The McKinley Years*, Solomon moved to substitute Dawes name for that of Brown's as official chairman of the 1900 convention. Dawes went on to win, the vote being 799-720.

Though there are many references to specific proceedings, the most important instances to note are those demonstrating Solomon's spirit, and just how deeply respected he was by all the men he worked with. Both Dawes and Cullom would make reference to seeking legal guidance from Solomon throughout their tenure in the Republican Party. Solomon was not only an adviser to Dawes, Cullom, and countless other Illinois state figures. His relationships went well beyond the political and professional; he was also a friend.

Dawes wrote that on the day of May 26, 1901 he arrived in Dixon and met Solomon and C.H. Hughes at the depot. They were also joined by Jules Lumbard, the most well-known patriotic singer of the era. As recorded in the book, *Stories of Great National Songs*, Jules and his brother Frank, known as "the great singers of the war," were the first to sing the "Battle Cry of Freedom" in 1861, just after President Abraham Lincoln announced the second call for Union troops in the Civil War. The song was written by George F. Root.

Though a white-haired veteran in 1901, Jules was still singing, and performed "America" at the Palmyra Cemetery in memory of the soldiers who had died in the war. The events of the day, clearly in celebration of Memorial Day although the popular holiday name hadn't quite caught on yet, were in the charge of the Grand Army of the Republic, and the crowd was so large that the ceremony took place outside in the cemetery instead of the church.

That evening, Dawes, along with Solomon, Judge Farrand, and a few other local politicians had dinner at Page farm, which is now the area known as Elks Page Park. They were the guests of Mr. Hughes. Also at the dinner was Benjamin F. Shaw, of the "newspaper Shaws" [the newspaper Shaws, publishers of the *Telegraph* were not related to Katherine's family] of Dixon. B.F. Shaw is also credited as one of the founders of the Republican Party, alongside Abraham Lincoln. Indeed, it was quite a cast of historically significant politicians and local business men. A final mention of Solomon in Dawes' journal was recorded later on May 26, 1901, where he wrote of having dinner with him in Dixon.

President McKinley would be assassinated less than four months later. Dawes was among McKinley's family, and a few others at the Milford home, where the President died. He had been there for six of the seven days that McKinley struggled to survive, and on September 13th, Dawes went into the President's room, after the family had left, and said a prayer for his deceased friend.

Clearly, Solomon had many influential friends, not only in Dixon, but in Springfield and Washington D.C. as well, which all led to his relationship with Theodore "Teddy" Roosevelt.

The McKinley and Roosevelt Years ~
Solomon's Appointment to Federal Judge

Theodore Roosevelt is unmistakably one of the darlings of the American Presidency. He was charismatic, enjoyed hunting, not only for sport, but in the name of science as the devout naturalist who would go on to create and champion our National Park System. Roosevelt took his friendships and government responsibilities seriously. One of the friendships he established early-on in his own political career was with Solomon Bethea. The friendship began while in their state Legislatures, Roosevelt serving in New York.

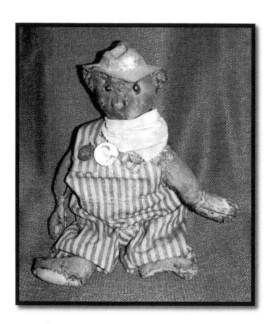

The original "Teddy Bear" was named for Roosevelt
This example from the period is complete with
Rough Rider hat/scarf and T.R. campaign button.
Photo by J. Thompson

In-fact, the political time-line of Roosevelt's rise in political esteem is remarkably similar to Solomon's. Both men declared their allegiance to the Republican Party in 1880, and both served in their respective State Legislatures in 1882 and 1883. It was during this time in the State Legislature that Solomon and Theodore became friends. In the book, *A Court That Shaped America: Chicago's Federal District Court From Abe Lincoln to Abbie Hoffman*, by Richard Cahan, appeared the following quote by author C. LeRoy Brown:

> "Mr. Roosevelt, it will be remembered, introduced in the New York legislature one of the earliest state civil service bills, and Mr. Bethea, after some correspondence with Mr. Roosevelt, introduced in the legislature of Illinois the same bill, which was the first measure ever offered in this state providing for civil service. This was the beginning of a long and close friendship between Roosevelt and Mr. Bethea."

Many letters were exchanged over the years, and in one letter dated September 6, 1901 regarding Roosevelt's growing support in Illinois, Solomon wrote, "I write to advise you that the result of your visit in Illinois is most satisfactory to your friends, and must be to you. I cannot see how conditions could be in better shape here for you. Everybody seems to be for you, and it seems to be so understood."

Solomon went on to write, "I noticed that in Englewood and Evanston they have started to organize Roosevelt Clubs. I have no doubt, if it is desired, there can be many of them organized. The question is as to whether it is too early. I would not

160

want to suggest anything in that line until further consideration and advice from you and your friends. If I can be of service to you in any way kindly advise me."

The letter was written on the same day President McKinley was shot, however it seems clear from the letter that it was written before Solomon had knowledge of the shooting. Since there is no mention of the assassination [at that time considered an attempt], one can surmise it was written early in the day before the shooting occurred.

Roosevelt wrote back on the 10th, saying, "Of course everything has been upset by this terrible attempt on the President's life. Now, however, he is out of danger...I think it is rather premature to start those clubs, but I do not exactly know what to do about stopping them. It seems to me to be a rather delicate matter to handle properly. I need not say how much I enjoyed seeing you and Stewart and Ames."

Roosevelt was referring to a breakfast he took with Solomon and others in late August. Solomon sent him a telegram inviting him to the breakfast, to which Roosevelt wrote back, "I am delighted to accept. Have anyone you wish. Will be at the Auditorium Annex."

The Auditorium Annex would go on to become The Congress Plaza Hotel, which was once known as the "Home of Presidents" among Chicago hotels, according to the hotel's history. It was considered the place where several Presidents rallied their partisans to discuss campaign strategies, and this telegram exchange is proof of this very occurrence.

~~~

Solomon was first appointed United States Attorney for the Northern District of Illinois by President McKinley in 1898, and would continue to work at the highest ranks in government. In 1905, President Roosevelt appointed him Federal Judge for the Illinois District. In fact, Solomon was considered the District's senior judge, and was appointed at the same time as Kenesaw Mountain Landis, who would later go on to become famous as the first commissioner of organized baseball.

It is easy to tell from the correspondence between the fellow-judges that they shared a strong friendship, and that Landis had an interesting sense of humor. In the earliest known letter written to Solomon, Landis wrote, "Dear Judge: Now you keep away from those courts. There is no possible necessity for your going to work. I am earnest about this. And you have earned it. Always your friend, Kenesaw M. Landis."

It seems perhaps that Solomon had taken ill, and Landis was encouraging him to take a break from all his hard work. However, after Landis closed the seemingly serious letter, he wrote at the bottom in large writing, "I am feeling like a prizefighter. KML." Perhaps this was his way as a fellow judge of offering to help with Solomon's work load.

Landis would of course write Solomon to discuss matters relating to the court, but most of the letters also reflect their genuine friendship rather than a business-as-usual relationship. In another letter, Landis wrote: "Dear Judge: Not a thing going on here—not a <u>single</u> thing. Stay where you are." From the correspondence, it seems as though Landis was often concerned about Solomon's well-being, and encouraged him to do as much work as possible from Dixon, and in one letter wrote, "If up North I will love to see you." Landis then scribed a little drawing of a whip, and underneath wrote, "The whip," and signed his name.

The letters are of interest as they show a friendship between Landis and Bethea that was not observed in their careers as judges. Solomon was considered the court's first senior judge, and Landis, 14 years younger, worked closely with Bethea, fulfilling the role of the district's new second judgeship. The two, though working closely together, were often considered opposites.

Author J.G. Taylor Spink, who wrote a biography of Landis in 1945, wrote "Though no one ever demanded greater respect for 'the Court' from arguing attorneys, witnesses and court attendants than Landis, some other judges threw up their hands in holy terror...They accused him of violating the dignity of the judiciary, and some of his most severe critics called him a buffoon, a mountebank, and a man who would do anything to make the front page."

Solomon Bethea was not among these "other judges" who spoke so badly of Landis, still they were viewed as starkly opposite in their approach to the handlings of the law. Bethea was described as having "simple, old-fashioned conceptions of public duty and he was sometimes rather unbending in the carrying out of such conceptions," wrote author C. LeRoy Brown. "But the bar respected his never failing purpose to act only as the law authorized him to act.

"His perception and understanding of the principals of the relationship between the government and the rights of individuals were in advance of the times, and he contributed largely

163

to the national movement to bring the great commercial interests of the country into subordination to the law," Brown wrote.

Before McKinley's assassination, Solomon and then Vice President Roosevelt began what would be a long professional relationship and enduring friendship. Since December of 1898, when Solomon was appointed as a United States District Attorney by President McKinley, he had spent a great deal of time in Chicago, much of the day-to-day business being carried out over lunches and dinners at The Chicago Club, and various other clubs of high-distinction in the city, and he stayed in close touch with Roosevelt.

Much of the correspondence between Solomon, The President and Vice-President, his fellow Judges and Senators was made through typed letters sent to and from his office in the Federal Building in Chicago. The Federal Building was a massive office building located on what was then the very south end of Chicago's commercial district. The building was and is today famous in architectural circles as The Monadnock. The Monadnock, located at 53 West Jackson Boulevard, upon its completion in 1892 was at this time considered the largest commercial structure in the world, and is today one of Chicago's great landmark buildings.

The Monadnock - Solomon's offices were here

From postal card published by Curt Teich & Co.

"The Monadnock is an achievement unsurpassed in the architectural history of our country. This building has no precedent in architecture; it is itself precedent. It comes up to an ideal, and by virtue of its correspondence with that ideal it becomes a work of art."

~ Robert Andrews, The *Architectural* Review, 1893.

What an exciting and demanding time it must have been for Solomon—acting in the highest ranks of governmental politics, in a city fast-growing amidst an era of un-relenting legal battles that spoke to the very core of Nation-wide industry, the assassination of President McKinley, and an appointment to the Federal Judiciary. On September 14, 1901, the day the President died, Solomon sent a telegram to Charles G. Dawes asking him to "Kindly advise about funeral arrangements. We want to see you there."

Still capture photo that may show Solomon Bethea (right)
with President Theodore Roosevelt (left) at the funeral
of President William McKinley in Canton, OH, 1901
"President Roosevelt at the Canton Station" Library of Congress,
Thomas A. Edison, 18 September 1901, H9085

The funeral procession was held a few days later in McKinley's hometown of Canton, Ohio, where he is buried at Westlawn Cemetery. The procession, copy written on film by

Thomas A. Edison, passed by the Canton Hardware Co. Wholesale building. Spectators were seen standing on the rooftops and awnings of nearly every building on the street. Footage was also taken of President Roosevelt arriving by train, as well as the funeral leaving the President's house and church. It is likely that Solomon appears somewhere in the footage, though a certain identification of him is impossible.

In a letter written to Charles Dawes after President McKinley's funeral, Solomon wrote, "After I had walked around McKinley's old home I did not feel like doing anything else." He wrote this in regard to not having met with Dawes in Canton, and invited him to Dixon instead to have dinner, no doubt at the Nachusa House. He also asked Dawes to stay the night in Dixon at his home. He wrote earlier in the letter, "I will not attempt to write you about any matters politically, but will wait until you come here which I understand will be the second of October." The tone of this letter suggests that Solomon had grown weary in light of McKinley's assassination, and his relationship with Roosevelt, now stepping into the President's shoes so to speak was bound to change. All of this had taken a toll on his health.

Solomon made a gift of $25 to the McKinley monument erected in Canton, and wrote in his letter that he regretted he could not send more money. This was not due to a lack of financial ability on Solomon's part, but because he was diligent and responsible with his money, as would be seen later when he made the considerable gift of the hospital to Dixon.

The stacks of surviving correspondence between Solomon and various politicians, including Charles Dawes, Shelby Cullom, and Theodore Roosevelt, among others, paints a picture of Solomon. The letters individually mostly pertain to business-as-usual, but there are a few that speak directly to Solomon's character.

An instance demonstrating Solomon's generosity and concern for the average citizen was seen in his correspondence with Charles Dawes in 1900. He wrote letters to Dawes concerning a Catherine J. Gilman, whose husband was killed in the Spanish War, asking for her promotion in the Census Office, where she was employed. He wrote, "I can assure you that nothing you could do for the heroes of the late war would be more fitting and proper than to look after the Gilman family. They are deserving in every way."

Catherine Gilman was eventually given the raise, and Solomon wrote letters of thanks to all the men involved in advancing her position in the Census Office. Beyond this specific example, a story of another sort is expressed in these letters. In spite of the drab political rhetoric, it is easy to see Solomon as he was—a good man. He took great care in composing each letter he sent, and his grammar was impeccable. Solomon was always gentle in the way he composed letters and used language. He chose words carefully, and it is obvious from reading only a few that Solomon genuinely cared about the men he worked with in Chicago and D.C.

In one letter, hand-written on Union League Club of Chicago stationary, dated January 27, 1899, Solomon wrote:

My Dear Mr. Dawes:

I beg leave to thank you for a copy of your annual report to Congress. I shall take great pleasure in perusing it as I have in considering your position upon many of the questions as to the currency.

I am,

Sir,

Very Respectfully,

S.H. Bethea

This was a common closing for Solomon, and though composition was much more proper and respectful than it is today, Bethea's letters demonstrate a certain commitment to courtesy and admiration. Each letter from Solomon clearly shows, rather than tells, that he cared deeply for everyone in his life—political or otherwise. Other closings include *Sincerely Yours, Very Truly Yours, Hoping to see you soon, I remain, very truly yours*, etc. He also consistently invited fellow politicians to dinners in Chicago and in Dixon, and often was the one who arranged them. He invited friends to stay with him at his home in Dixon or made arrangements for them to stay at the Nachusa House. Clearly Solomon was a lonely man, and took great pleasure in his professional relationships—he was not simply a professional lawyer and judge collecting a paycheck and accolades—his political life *was his life*.

Solomon and The Beef Trust

"If you counted with it the other big plants—and they were now really one—
...it was the greatest aggregation of labour and capital ever gathered in one
place."

~ Upton Sinclair, *The Jungle*, 1936

Undeniably, one of the largest industrial scandals in the early 20th Century was known as the "Beef Trust." All across the United States, packing houses were becoming suspect in their business dealings. This case included a number of serious issues relating to the huge meat-packing industry in Chicago. There were, of course, serious issues relating to migrant worker's rights and working conditions, the thoroughness and quality (or lack thereof) of meat inspections, and the price of meat, but the largest question was of *Swift & Company, Armor, and Morris* forming a virtual monopoly over the meat industry in thirteen major cities, when they formed the *National Packing Company.*

This prompted a federal antitrust investigation, of which Solomon Bethea in his role as United States District Attorney for the Northern District of Illinois was a major player. Solomon was involved from the very beginning of this investigation, securing one of the first injunctions against the National Packing Company. Working directly with two secret agents assigned to him by the Federal Bureau of Investigation, and with the support of President Roosevelt, Solomon was frequently making it onto the front page

170

of the *New York Times*, and his work has been recorded in many obscure histories that chronicle the early portions of the case.

Simply, these meat packers had violated the Sherman Antitrust Act of 1890, which was signed into law by President Benjamin Harrison. The Act was put in place as a means for the Federal government to investigate and pursue companies suspected of being in violation. It was the first statute set in place to limit the formation of monopolies and cartels.

As early as 1898 Solomon was looking into The Trust. His work would begin to gain public attention and the serious notice of the President in 1901, and would not reach final settlement until after Solomon's death. It was a case not to be taken lightly, and Solomon pursued the investigation vigorously. The case lingered for many years, being contested by the substantial resources of The Trust. Solomon's involvement in these initial investigations of The Trust made this small town lawyer from Dixon, now Federal Prosecutor, a major player in one of the Nation's biggest legal stories at the beginning of the 20th Century. Much of what Solomon began at that time has resulted today in the Food and Drug Administration and its broad powers to govern our food supply.

The Deaths of Generals:

Ulysses S. Grant

On July 23, 1885, General Ulysses S. Grant died in Mt. McGregor, New York. For the next several days the *Telegraph* would report on Grant's death, beginning with the headline, "The Night is Past. Our 'Old Commander' answers the roll-call." Despite "hypodermic injections of brandy…to stimulate the flagging strength" given to Grant throughout the night of the 22nd, he died at 8:09 in the morning.

New York was actually Grant's third choice for a final resting place. His first choice was West Point, but because his wife, Julia Dent, could not join him there, he wrote that he wanted to be buried in Galena, Illinois, where he lived for many years. He wrote his burial wishes down on a slip of paper, which was given to his son, writing his final wishes as such:

"Galena, or some other place in Illinois—because from that state I received my first general's commission. New York—because the people of that city befriended me in my need."

His son tore the note up only hours before his father died, saying to him, "I don't like any of it. There is no need of talking of such things." His doctors suggested he died of "sheer exhaustion," though Grant had been told he was suffering from throat cancer.

On the 24th, a meeting was held at the Lee County Court House, at the request of the mayor, Judge Farrand. Solomon was appointed to sit on the general committee organizing General Grant's funeral rites given in Dixon. Solomon helped to secure his friend Emery A. Storrs, a well-known lawyer of Chicago, to eulogize Grant.

Storrs, known as "the great orator," arrived in Dixon on August eighth, to a crowd of thousands gathered on the court house lawn. The city of Dixon had been "draped in mourning" since the news of Grant's death, the committee having requested all local businesses to drape the windows of their establishments from 2:00 to 5:00 p.m. every day. The service was a lengthy one, Mayor Farrand speaking at-length first, and introducing Storrs, who as expected, delivered a long, eloquent speech. Storrs began by telling the people of Dixon that he was impressed by how much the small city had grown in the years it had been since he was last there—not only in size, but in political affiliation and progress. Solomon, with his significant political and organizational skills, was clearly a large part of this observation and the success of the memorial event.

He closed his eulogy with the following:

"His spirit is to-day enrolled among the immortals; his name will stand forever upon our national records a part of the priceless treasures of the great names of American history, and if the heavens could open this day, surely we could see standing there side by side, Washington, Lincoln and Grant, breathing blessings upon the land they loved so much and so dearly; and as we gaze upon those transfigured spirits, and before the skies shall close, with uncovered heads and unshod feet we reverently hail and salute them."

John A. Logan

Two years later, Illinois native and esteemed General of the Union Army, John A. Logan died on December 27, 1887. Solomon and Logan were both in Springfield in 1882 and 1883, Solomon in the House of Representatives and Logan serving in the Senate. John A. Logan was also an attorney for the Third District of Illinois in 1858 and 1860. Solomon and General Logan no doubt crossed paths countless times, having both attended the Republican conventions, and probably dined together in Chicago on many occasions.

The City of Dixon organized obsequies for Logan's death just as it had for Grant's. The principal eulogy was delivered by Reverend J.M. Ruthrauff, and Colonel H.T. Noble, A.C. Bardwell, as well as Solomon Bethea would deliver speeches. The service, which was sponsored by the Dixon Post No. 299 of G.A.R., was held at the Opera House on Sunday, January 3, 1887 at 2:30 that afternoon [The Opera House would burn down in 1920, and The Dixon Theatre was rebuilt at the same location]. The Dixon Ladies Quartet sang a hymn, and then the speakers took the stage.

Unfortunately, Solomon Bethea's speech was not transcribed in the paper. Solomon was the last to take the stage, "with earnest and eloquent remarks which we are unable to give to-day for lack of both time and space." The *Dixon Sun* criticized the *Telegraph* for not publishing the speech, which was explained on January 7th, saying, "The other speakers at the Logan obsequies prepared their speeches and by request the manuscripts were furnished the *Telegraph*; but Mr. Bethea's address was extemporaneous and therefore we were unable to procure a report, at least in time for publication in our *Weekly*, where we desired the entire proceedings, and so omitted it entirely. The speech was highly praised generally by those who heard it."

One quote from Solomon from the speech, as reported by the *Dixon Sun*, which may or may not have been accurate, was, "General Logan was a statesman because his bravery made him one." The *Dixon Sun* interpreted this statement as Solomon suggesting that his idea of statesmanship might be found in a prize fighter. The *Telegraph* interpreted this quote as Solomon "clearly stating that General Logan took a deep interest in looking after the good of the people and endeavored to frame laws for their benefit, thus acting the part of a statesman."

Regardless of Solomon's impromptu speech being lost to history, judging by all the addresses he had made that were reported, and his speeches in the courtroom as recorded in the proceedings of the Thiel trial of 1886, surely he delivered a moving and heart-felt closing for the Logan memorial in Dixon on that Sunday in 1887.

Solomon liked a good "Quote"

Throughout his life Solomon was known for his oratorical skills and was, as often seen in this book, known to quote verse and prose to make a point or to demonstrate his core beliefs.

In fact, a pamphlet came to light that was produced in Dixon in 1898 called *Favorite Quotations of Dixon People*. It was published by and produced as a "W.R.C. Souvenir." The W.R.C. was the "Women's Relief Corp" a sister organization to the Grand Army of the Republic (G.A.R.) the veteran's organization for those who served the Union forces during the Civil War.

It is likely that this pamphlet was produced for distribution during one of the many G.A.R. reunions that were held throughout the post-war period in places like Dixon. G.A.R. reunions were a time for remembrance and reflection and there was often much speech-making. To have a book of inspirational and motivational quotes from local leading citizens was a natural for a souvenir.

According to the website *Illinois in the Civil War*, The Grand Army of the Republic was founded in Decatur, Illinois in 1866 and was the largest organization of Union veterans of the Civil war and remained active until 1956. They promoted comradeship, assisted survivors and their families and maintained old soldier's homes. In its heyday around 1890 the G.A.R. had 409,000 members, mostly steadfast Republicans. They were also involved in establishing "Old Settlers" groups like the one that operated in Dixon and Lee County. Dixon's Old Settlers held their own annual celebrations during the same time period as the G.A.R. and the W.R.C.

General John Alexander Logan was the commander in chief of the Illinois G.A.R. and inaugurated the observance of Memorial Day to honor fallen soldiers in 1868. There were many opportunities for Solomon to show off his speaking abilities and his fondness for quoting an appropriate verse.

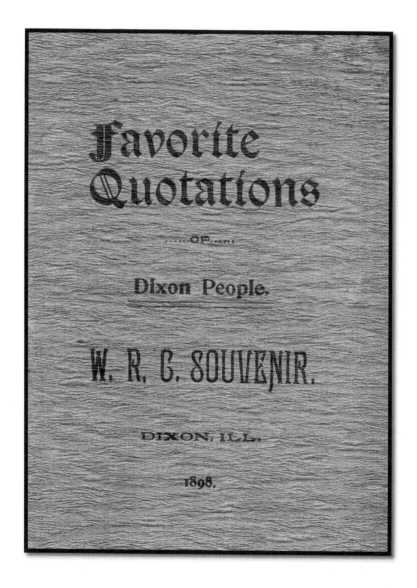

Favorite Quotations

.....OF.....

Dixon People.

W. R. C. SOUVENIR.

DIXON, ILL.

1898.

NINA THOMPSON,

"In the moral life conscience predominates"

JAS. H. THOMPSON,

"A man that can render a reason, is a man worthy of an answer; but he that argueth for victory, deserveth not the tenderness of Trouble."

S. H. BETHEA,

Hold her nozzle agin the bank 'till the last galoot's ashore.

—*John Hay*

E. S. WOODBRIDGE,

In this the act of living lies,
To want no more that may suffice;
And make that little do.

—*Cotton*

A little learning is a dangerous thing,
Drink deep or taste not the Pierian spring,
There shallow draughts intoxicate the
    brain,
But drinking largely, sobers us again.

—*Pope*

JANE ROBINS,

"Late to bed and early to rise,
Prepares a man for his home in the skies."

E. C. CROPSEY,

There may be heaven—there must be hell;
Meantime, there is our life here. We-ell.

—*Rudyard Kipling*

Solomon's quote here from John Hay in the 1898 W.R.C. Souvenir *Favorite Quotes of Dixon People* is from the poem *Jim Bludso of the Prairie Belle*. If you read the poem and understand as Solomon did that this is the voice of Lincoln speaking about being steadfast, and written by Lincoln's former secretary, you can see that it matches up precisely with Solomon and his actions and opinions. He did, in fact, "*Hold her nozzle agin the bank*" throughout his life.

Jim Bludso of the Prairie Belle

WELL, no, I can't tell where he lives,
Because he don't live, you see.
　　Leastways, he's got out of habit
Of livin' like you and me.
　　Oh, where have you been these last three year,
That you havn't heard folks tell
　　How Jimmie Bludso passed in his checks
The night of the Prairie Belle?

　　He weren't no saint -- them engineers
Are pretty much alike --
　　One wife in Natchez under the Hill,
And another one here, in Pike.
　　A careless man in his talk was Jim,
And an awkward hand in a row,
　　But he never flunked and he never lied, --
I reckon he never knowed how.

　　And this was all the religion he had, --
To treat his engine well;
　　Never be passed on the river;
To mind the pilot's bell.
　　And if ever the Prairie Belle took fire, --
A thousand times he swore
　　He'd hold her nozzle agin the bank
Till the last soul got ashore.

　　All boats have their day on the Mississip,

179

And her day come at last. --
    The Movastar was a better boat,
But the Belle she *wouldn't* be passed.
    And so she came tearing along that night,
The oldest craft on the line --
    With a crewman squat on her safety valve
And her furnace crammed, rosin and pine.

    And the fire broke out as she cleared the bar,
And burned a hole in the night,
    And quick as a flash she turned, and made
For the willer-bank on the right.
    There was runnin' and cursin', but Jim yelled
    out,
Over all the infernal roar,
    "I'll hold her nozzle agin the bank
Till the last galoot's ashore."

    Through the hot, black breath of the burning
    boat
Jim Bludso's voice was heard,
    And they all had faith in his cussedness,
And knowed he would keep his word.
    And, sure as you're born, they all got off
Before the smokestacks fell, --
    And Bludso's ghost went up alone
In the smoke of the Prairie Belle.

    He weren't no saint, but at Judgement
I'd run my chance with Jim,
    'Longside of some pious gentlemen
That wouldn't shake hands with him.
    He seen his duty, a dead sure thing, --
And he went for it, thar and then,
    And Christ ain't a going to be too hard
On a man that died for men.

~ **John Hay**

"John Hay, formerly one of Lincoln's private secretaries was later Secretary of State under McKinley and Roosevelt. In a pamphlet with another ballad, "Little Breeches," Hay's *Jim Bludso*...poem was immediately popular and widely reprinted throughout the U.S. and England and was later included in the collection *Pike County Ballads*, the title referring to Hay's home county in Illinois, bordering the Mississippi River. His instant literary success put him on the same lyceum circuit with Mark Twain, Harriet Beecher Stowe and Horace Greeley.

According to musician Dave Para who has put the poem to song, in Tyler Dennett's 1933 biography of Hay, "Dennett said, 'Jim Bludso,' in the facile words of John Hay, is the voice of Abraham Lincoln, the kind of story he would have liked to tell, the kind of a moral he would have liked to point."

Solomon Rejoins Katherine

"Solie is well off but he looked sad at times when he got to talking about the folks. Wealth don't make happiness."
~ Aunt Margaret Bethea, letter, October 23, 1905

It is utterly remarkable that Solomon accomplished so much during his career and various political appointments, all the while doting on Katherine and worrying constantly about her health. As noted in the chapter about Katherine, Solomon frequently accompanied her on her convalescent trips to Colorado, New Mexico and North Carolina.

Long after "Kittie" passed away, "Solie" loved his best girl. It may seem archaic, a bit over-romantic to say it as such, but Solomon Hicks Bethea surely lived his life-entire for Katherine Campbell Shaw—and she was someone upon whom everyone she met made an impression. She loved this man well enough single-handedly for him to make his last wishes that of gifting a hospital in her name to the people and growing city of Dixon.

Solomon died on August 3, 1909 at approximately 12:40 a.m. in Sterling at the home of his cousin, S.S. Royer. He was only 57 years old. Few people come anywhere close to achieving Solomon's accomplishments with the gift of a full lifetime. Solomon was raised to know the value of hard work by his father, who had also suffered a lonesome life peppered with familial loss. It is clear why Solomon threw himself so lovingly into his career—really, after Katherine, it was all he had.

The cause of death was recorded as "Exhaustion due to chronic nephritis." According to *The Merck Manual*, nephritis is an inflammatory disease of the kidneys. Essentially he died of kidney failure, and in local papers it was recorded as *Bright's disease*, which is a group of "diffused bilateral nonsuppurative diseases" of the kidneys.

Solomon had suffered from various complications since at least September of 1906, with the onset of his health problems being bladder trouble. A few days before his death, the *Telegraph* made record of the illness as it slowly progressed over the years. He had suffered from rheumatism for many years, now a colloquial term which most likely simply meant that he suffered from some form of arthritis. In April of 1909 he suffered an attack of ptomaine poisoning, which was the term used at the time to describe food poisoning, and was rushed to Chicago's St. Luke's Hospital. This certainly aggravated any underlying health conditions he had.

There are many details of Solomon's travels in the *Telegraph* report which do not appear anywhere else in various documents, though it is clear that he was always on the go, and rarely stayed in one place for very long. According to the article, Solomon, when first taken ill, spent a considerable amount of time convalescing at the Palmyra farm where he no doubt rode the horses as often as possible if his health permitted. In November of 1906 he was stable enough to go to Chicago for an X-Ray, the technology having been around for not much more than 10 years. There it was confirmed that he had a large stone in his bladder, which was no doubt unbelievably painful, and required surgery.

At that time Solomon was in no shape for the operation though, so he made his way south to Gulfport, Mississippi where he spent the winter. The operation was successfully completed at St. Luke's Hospital in Chicago that March. After recovering for a number of weeks in the hospital, Solomon returned to Dixon for the summer, again staying at the farm. In October he returned to Chicago and held court all winter. In June of 1908 it was reported that he sailed from New York to Europe for a six-week vacation.

The last year of his life, was spent between Dixon and Chicago, where he was confined once more to St. Luke's Hospital for several weeks. Solomon was comatose for the last few days of his life, regaining consciousness for only brief moments when he would recognize the Royer family attending him in Sterling. He lost complete consciousness Sunday, August first, and remained unconscious until his death in early morning the following Tuesday.

The funeral train, consisting of one interurban and a wagon, made its way slowly from Sterling to Dixon. As the train passed through Palmyra, men working in the fields stopped work and took off their hats "out of respect for the memory of one whom all loved to honor and whom all admired." At each farmhouse families gathered at the roadside in silence to watch as the train crept passed carrying the fresh-cut flower adorned coffin of their good friend, "Sol" H. Bethea.

Solomon's passing shook not only the City of Dixon, but reverberated all the way to Washington D.C. as a swath of mourners began to emerge. President Roosevelt, unable to attend the funeral, appointed a committee of 12 to travel to Dixon. The line-up of United States politicians was long. Among those in attendance were Solomon's dear friend and fellow judge, Kenesaw Mountain Landis, and Judges John Barton Payne and Peter S. Grosscup.

Also in attendance were Internal Revenue Service Collector Henry L. Hertz; former U.S. District Attorney Thomas Milchrist; U.S. District Attorney Edward W. Sims; Assistant District Attorneys Ben Davis and J.W. Wilderson; Attorney Elwood G. Goodman; Clerk of the District Court T.C. McMillan; Clerk of the United States Circuit Court, Mr. Stoddard; United States Marshall, Luman T. Hoy and his Deputy W.D. Mack; Sub-Treasurer of the U.S. Treasury William Baldenweck; Deputy U.S. Clerk C.J. Bentley; Post Office Inspectors Henry D. Dement and I.T. Mullin; U.S. Commissioner Mark Foote; Representative J.H. Gray, Ex-Senator Delos Baxter, representatives of The State Bar Association, and many others from around Lee County. In all, thousands of mourners arrived in Dixon to honor the late judge.

Reverend Whitcombe delivered a prayer and he read Chapter 4 of the First Thessalonians. An excerpt follows:

"But I would not have you to be ignorant, brethren, concerning them which are asleep, that ye sorrow not, even as others which have no hope. For if we believe that Jesus died and rose again, even so them also which sleep in Jesus will God bring with him. For this we say unto you by the word of the Lord, that we which are alive and remain unto the coming of the Lord shall not prevent them which are asleep. For the Lord himself shall descend from heaven with a shout, with the voice of the archangel, and with the trump of God: and the dead in Christ shall rise first: Then we which are alive and remain shall be caught up together with them in the clouds, to meet the Lord in the air: and so

shall we ever be with the Lord. Wherefore comfort one another with these words."

After the reading from the scripture, Ella Richards, a noted vocalist from Sterling, sang *In The Sweet By and By*, a hymn written by Samuel F. Bennett and J.P. Webster in 1868. The hymn was a favorite throughout the country, and no doubt many in attendance knew the words by heart. The lyrics follow:

There's a land that is fairer than day,
And by faith we can see it afar;
For the Father waits over the way
To prepare us a dwelling place there.

In the sweet (in the sweet)
By and by (by and by)
We shall meet on that beautiful shore;
In the sweet (in the sweet)
By and by (by and by)
We shall meet on that beautiful shore.

We shall sing on that beautiful shore
The melodious songs of the blest,
And our spirits shall sorrow no more
Not a sigh for the blessing of rest.
To our bountiful father above
We will offer our tribute of praise;
For the glorious gift of His love
And the blessings that hallow our days.

186

Hearing of Solomon's death, Shelby Cullom sent a telegram, then published in the *Telegraph*. It read:

This moment received telegram announcing death of Judge Bethea. My heart is so full of sorrow I have not words to express it. Few minutes ago had just dictated letter to you expressing hope that he might live and recover his health, although since your telegram of a few days ago there seemed little ground for hope. Judge Bethea was one of the purest and best men I ever knew. Until his health failed he was proving himself to be an able federal judge. Had he lived he would have made a great record on the bench, a record that would have been an honor to our state and country. He was my personal friend for many years. I loved him as a brother and was proud to have the pleasure of recommending his appointment on the federal bench. Regret exceedingly that condition of my health is such that I am unable to take the trip to Dixon to attend the funeral.

There are two letters written to Solomon, one in 1906 and one in 1907 expressing concern for his health and providing evidence that his health had been failing, or at least fluctuating for a number of years before his death. The first letter, written at The Nachusa House on Nachusa House stationary, came from James H. Eckels, the Comptroller of the Currency of the United States, on October 3, 1906. It reads as follows:

My Dear Judge,

I am spending the afternoon with the Brintons and have come to the Hotel for a minute simply to leave you a note with respect that you are ill and to express the hope that you will speedily be fully well again.

With Expressions Great and Very Sincerely,

James H. Eckels

187

The second letter came from Charles Dawes, written on The Chicago Club stationary dated April 17, 1907. It reads as follows:

My Dear Sol:

I am so glad to hear that you are doing so well that I am dropping you this line to tell you so. Your friends have not forgotten you in your illness and we will be delighted to see you again in your accustomed vigor. Hurry up join us. Peters is still making salad.

Your Friend,

Charles G. Dawes

There were a number of sentiments recorded in the *Telegraph* in November of 1909 when The Dixon Bar Association held a memorial for Solomon. Several aspects of his life, and the impression he made upon his fellow attorneys were reported, beginning with a brief sketch of his life and it was noted that he was well-read.

"He was a lover of good literature and possessed that breadth of business and legal knowledge, which is acquired by much reading, and by a thorough intimacy with the great authors and writers of the past, as well as the great thinkers of the present day."

C. B. Morrison said, "Judge Bethea was a remarkable man, a friend to everybody, loyal to the bar and loyal to his people. He was a good citizen wherever he lived, always an honorable and upright man. He was a believer in a living God. He was a church man and a devout believer in church forms. He was a born leader of men. It was natural for him to command men, and men naturally followed him."

J. F. Palmer said of Solomon, "Judge Bethea seemed to have the faculty of saying the right thing at the right time to make all comfortable. He possessed qualities that make strong men."

Not an ill word was ever spoken of Solomon, even his perceived political adversaries had good things to say about him. The picture painted of Solomon through countless documents is undeniable: He was a gentle, kind, considerate man of immense intelligence who would dine with Presidents, and could just as easily take the shirt off of his back and give it to a man in need. These rare qualities are still appreciated to this day, and made a lasting impression on the City of Dixon. When his will was read it became public that he had bequeathed his estate for use in the construction of a Dixon hospital, something Katherine desperately needed, but did not have ready access to, something, much like St. Luke's, that offered the treatments that had kept him alive and well long after a string of illnesses would have surely cut his life even shorter. The hospital is the Shaw-Bethea legacy to their community.

Solomon's Gift ~ Katherine Shaw Bethea Hospital

"Judge Bethea left no near relatives."

~ Dixon Telegraph

Solomon's work on establishing Katherine Shaw Bethea Hospital began as early as 1895, when the City Council approved the ordinance for the non-sectarian public hospital on November 1st. It was also established at this time that the hospital was to have a board of nine women to be appointed by the mayor. Katherine's Sister Elizabeth would serve on the board, and remained closely tied to the hospital's operation until her death in 1910.

In 1896 the hospital had 12 beds, and would grow exponentially throughout the years, and continues to do so today. Solomon's final will and testament, which was written in 1907, was filed in the probate court and published in the *Telegraph* on August 6, 1909. With the exception of his law library, which was willed to George C. Dixon, Solomon bequeathed nearly his entire estate to the hospital, which inventoried at between $100,000 and $125,000—excerpts follow:

"I, Solomon Hicks Bethea, of Dixon, Lee County, Illinois, being of sound and disposing mind and memory do make, publish and declare this my last will and testament, hereby revoking all former wills, testaments and codicils by me at any time heretofore made."

Between willing his law library and other books, valued at some $9,000, and another $1,500 to the up-keep of both the

191

Bethea and Shaw cemetery plots, the final balance was to go to the hospital—making the final sum going to the hospital to be between $85,000 and $105,000. Solomon's will, in regard to the hospital, is written as follows:

"Fifth, I give, devise and bequeath all the rest residue and remainder of my estate, personal and mixed, to the Board of Directors of the Dixon Public Hospital, otherwise known as Katherine Shaw Bethea Hospital of Dixon, Illinois, and their successors in office, for the sole use and benefit of said Hospital forever, for the purposes thereof, and it is my desire that this devise and bequest and the income there from shall be used as far as is practicable to assist in the care of the needy sick and unfortunate of the Townships of Palmyra and Dixon...and that said persons shall be admitted to said Hospital free of charge as far as in the judgment of the Board of Directors of said Hospital it is practicable so to do and will not in any way impair the financial condition of said Hospital.

"Sixth, it is my will that the said Hospital shall be called Katherine Shaw Bethea Hospital and that the names of my father, William Wilson Bethea, and of my mother, Emily Green Bethea, shall always be connected with said Hospital, or some portion thereof, so that this devise and bequest shall be a memorial to all three of them."

With this money set in place, KSB Hospital began to grow. Little more than a year later, Elizabeth Shaw, Katherine's sister, who served as the Director of the hospital's board, passed away. She, too, willed the larger balance of her estate to the hospital, which included the real estate and proceeds of two farms, and

192

approximately $30,000, $6,000 of which was to be used to maintain a "free bed" to be used to provide medical attention for any person in need who could not pay, and when a bed was available. Elizabeth also requested that two rooms or wards be named one in honor of her sister, Katherine and one in honor of Solomon's mother, Emily Green.

Only once did the financial stability of KSB ever come into possible danger when, in 1912, Elizabeth's surviving brothers William and Samuel Shaw challenged the wills of Elizabeth and Mary, stating that they were not of sound mind when their wills were made. The complaint was dismissed; however both brothers were awarded $2,500.

There are two letters that speak directly to Katherine's health and the creation of the hospital written between Elizabeth and Solomon in 1907. They show the absolute devastating emotional force behind the creation of the hospital. In Elizabeth's letter, some of which is nearly indecipherable, she wrote:

"Dear Sollie, Your letter this morning brought me some thing as near joy as I have known in these fourteen sad years and I thank God that my prayers that you might some time realize just what you say has been answered. If they in heaven can and do know what is done on earth then Kittie is indeed happy. There are many things she said to me that last night which you made it impossible for me to tell you and no one else could hear them. I know now that you are more sinned against than sinning that you can wind a whip of thorns to scourge me and there was none brave enough to show you the truth by telling you what your best friends said. Perhaps the time may come when I can tell you of those last hours. They have burdened all these years for me.

A braver more unselfish soul never lived and suffered without complaint. I have been reading and burning her letters, a thing that has wrung my heart but after this sickness feel that it must be done, might not be able if another attack comes. Only one single line in them all sours of a complaint reads "I wonder why these people can't call in court this forum themselves and let Sollie come back to me." Another tells of the awful desolation that comes when you are gone and the trunks place empty but adds 'I shall be all right soon and everybody is kind.' The Christmas letter tells of all the courtesies received and that she reads her Bible in the shadow of the mountain with new light on the words."

This letter clearly shows how much Katherine loved Solomon and missed him when he was away on business or when she was at various tuberculosis sanitariums, and that she confessed these feelings in letters to her sister rather than to Solomon directly, no doubt as to not worry or burden him.

In the surviving letter Solomon wrote to Elizabeth he deals directly with the business of the hospital. He wrote:

"I have never talked with anyone about the naming of the hospital. You know from the plans that I have made that I would be pleased if the directors could of their own accord call the hospital what I direct shall be done some time." He went on to write, *"Do not worry about the hospital or write about it—we will talk it over when I come. I shall do nothing to interfere with your plans, or with the Board doing what you desire."*

194

Clearly Solomon wanted Elizabeth to have full control over all matters concerning the hospital; which through her hard and diligent work while he was in Chicago fulfilling his duties as District Attorney and as Federal Judge, flourished under her careful management.

~~~

There is no better way to remark on Solomon's integrity and the effect he had on each individual in his life, than to simply quote the words of L.H. Jennings as written in Solomon's biographical sketch in the *University of Michigan Alumni Record*: "Though we say, 'He is dead,' he is not dead, for he lives in the lives and hearts of those who knew him." Jennings' sentiment could not be more accurate.

Solomon was also remembered with much esteem in the *Report of the Thirty-Third Annual Meeting of the American Bar Association of 1910*:

"Judge Bethea was a man of high character and strong convictions, and throughout his public career was inspired by a sincere purpose to do his duty as he saw it."

Solomon continues to touch the lives and hearts of the living each day, as the gift he began in 1895, Katherine Shaw Bethea Hospital, remains as a testament to his commitment to the every-man, his community, and the love of his life—an all-but-simple farm girl folks called, *Kittie*.

Katherine Shaw Bethea Hospital

Early view...

The original hospital opened in 1897
a gift of Solomon Hicks Bethea
in memory of his wife
Katherine Campbell Shaw Bethea
and his parents.

In later years as the hospital grew
elements of the original building
were incorporated as part of
KSB Hospital because the facilities
quite literally grew around it.

Dixon's Proposed Hospital-A Much Needed Donation.

THE TELEGRAPH has for years talked much and frequently urged the actual necessity (for it is not a luxury) of a hospital of some sort in this city. Dixon has now advanced to such a position among the cities of the state and the nation as to make it necessary to be abreast of the times and at least respectable, that there shall be in the city limits a place where strangers among us meeting with an accident, or taken suddenly ill, may be cared for as they could not be at the present time in any public house. Where, indeed, our own citizens who may require severe and precarious operations can be treated scientifically and in many respects much more comfortably than even at their homes. Thus it will be understood that no more noble charity could have been rendered this people than that which comes from our fellow citizen, Hon. S. H. Bethea, in assuring to Dixon such an institution as we have alluded to above. Mr. Bethea has purchased the house and lot, corner of First street and Dixon avenue, being the southwest quarter of block one, from Mrs. Jas. H. Thompson and donated the perpetual use of the same to the city for a hospital. We hope that the city council will so appreciate this most worthy and thoughtful charity as to at once place the building in readiness for patients. It is a beautiful spot, with a charming view of Rock River, the island and great scope of the valley, and no more appropriate place could be selected for such a charitable purpose. The house with its porches and pleasant surroundings can, with but little work, be placed in readiness for the most excellent purpose designed.

The Telegraph account of the purchase/gift of property for a public hospital for Dixon from Hon. S. H. Bethea

Solomon Hicks Bethea Home

Residence of Hon. Solomon Hicks Bethea and
Katherine Campbell Shaw Bethea
at 314 South Ottawa Avenue.

This home was designed by Joseph Lyman Silsbee
a prominent Chicago architect and
mentor to Frank Lloyd Wright.

Silsbee designed the home in his Queen Anne style
similar to that of Katherine's brother James A. Shaw's
home in Mount Carroll, Illinois.

Shaw's home remained largely unaltered
unlike the Solomon Bethea home.
The Bethea home was significantly changed
and remodeled in the 1990's when
it was used by Lee County
for a juvenile justice facility.

Elizabeth and Anna Shaw Home

Residence of Katherine's mother and sisters
Elizabeth and Mary Anna Shaw.

Although referred to in this account
as located on North Ottawa Avenue,
the home today is addressed on East Chamberlin Street.

It may be assumed that Katherine spent her final days here
and passed away March 22, 1893 in this home
with her sister Elizabeth in attendance
as indicated in Elizabeth's letter to Solomon
cited on page 193 in this book.

Katherine's funeral was also held in this home
prior to her interment at Oakwood Cemetery.

Endnotes

It should be explained that for the purposes of writing this book consideration was given to the style of writing that could best convey the book's purpose. The book started out to be a historical double biography but somewhere along the way became a love story as the author learned more about her subjects.

To avoid intrusive use of footnoting and formal referencing, source materials are noted, explained and attributed throughout the text in such a way as to give proper credit without interfering with the flow of the story. The author hopes this helps the reader to accomplish a primary goal of the book and that is to get to know Solomon Hicks and Katherine Shaw Bethea as people.

Many of the images and illustrations herein are used as reminders of times past and as ways to look at the characters through the window of our imaginations. They are often old photographs that for many readers will show both in a literal sense how people and things looked; but in addition, ask important questions related to just who the subjects were.

The arts, including literature, ask questions, provide some answers and leave others matters unanswered. This book does each of these.

A.K. Thompson is a writer and musician. She holds a BS in Journalism from SIUC, a Master's Degree in Writing and Consciousness from the New College of California, and an MFA in Creative Writing Fiction from Southern Illinois University, where she also taught English composition and technical writing. She sings the part of a ghostly banjo on the album *Long Term Plan* by The Whistle Pigs. She served as Assistant Editor for the *Crab Orchard Review* literary magazine for the 2009 and 2010 editions. She is published in *The Smoking Poet, The Chiron Review,* and writes a monthly column *"Dirt Church,"* for *Adventure Sports Outdoors Magazine.* Her short fiction *The Taxidermist* is included in *Surreal South '11,* the third of a series of southern flavored anthologies from *Press 53.* Thompson was born in KSB Hospital Dixon, Illinois.